HAUTE AS IN OAT

HAUTE AS IN OAT

A Pronunciation Guide to the
Cuisines and Wines of
France, Germany and Italy

Wilfred J. McConkey

Madison Books
Lanham • New York • London

Library of Congress Cataloging-in-Publication Data

McConkey, Wilfred J.
Haute as in oat.

1. Cookery, European—Terminology—Pronunciation.
2. Wine and wine making—Europe—Terminology—
Pronunciation. I. Title.
TX644.M38   1988   641.594'014   88–13191
ISBN 0–8191–6823–5 (alk. paper)
ISBN 0–8191–6824–6 (pbk. : alk. paper)

Contents

Foreword

Haute as in Oat is intended to serve as something more than a survival manual for Americans foraging for food and drink in Europe or Manhattan's Upper East Side.

To the extent that printed instructions can elicit pleasing pronunciations—or, at least ones that don't offend the native ear—this guide strives to provide them. Because some key sounds in French and German aren't used in English, directions for reproducing these sounds are provided.

A restaurant reviewer observed recently that when it comes to food Americans talk French but eat Italian. Because this guide deals with what we say, not just what we savor, the French section is comparatively large.

There are other reasons for its disproportionate size. Not only have that nation's chefs been prodigiously inventive, they tended to give their creations fanciful titles *(á l'Ambassadrice, Chambord)*. German and Italian chefs have been more definitive, often naming theirs after the ingredients or cooking methods that distinguish them. And, if the pronunciations for these ingredients and methods are provided elsewhere in the guide, the creation isn't listed separately. *Zuppa di Piselli e Vongole*, for instance, isn't included in soups because the ingredients and their pronunciations appear in other categories—*piselli* under Vegetables and *vongole* under Fish, Shellfish and Mollusks.

The standard set for pronunciations in this guide is that they be readily acceptable to knowledgeable Americans.

Why not choose Florentines, Berliners and Parisians as arbiters? Because there is no way of grouping letters on paper to capture their idiosyncratic intonations, cadences, ellipses, compressions and attenuations.

Are knowledgeable Americans more toler-
ant? On the contrary, people who are fluent in
a second language are usually zealous guard-
ians of its integrity. But, having painstakingly
mastered another tongue they understand the
special problems it poses for Americans.

The "knowledgeable Americans" who served
as my sources and board of review are all
fluent in one or more of the subject languages.

We had little or no disagreement over the
proper pronunciation of words, but plenty
about how best to convey them to the reader.
The French sauce, *Béarnaise,* sparked a fairly
typical dispute—for which three different
solutions were suggested, each with its own
logic and merits. Its three syllables can be
represented as bay-ar-**nez**. The French tele-
scope the first two into something that sounds
to the untrained ear very much like bear—
but not quite. If you go with bear-**nez** you
make it easy to say and remember, but you
lose a flicker of sound. If you isolate each
syllable to capture all the sounds the reader
may say it the same way, with awkward results.
We compromised with bay-ar**nez**.

In cases where elaborate analogues would
be required to convey all the nuances of
the word I settled, arbitrarily, for simple unam-
biguous instructions—and small impurities.

Another area of contention was the extent
to which Americanization merited recognition.
In other words, how many wrongs make a
right?

Hors-d'oeuvre is a case in point. It's pronounced "or derves" by most Americans, chefs
included. Does that legitimatize this pronunciation for domestic consumption? We agreed it
did, but that the reader would be better
served—perhaps literally so in Paris—with the
French pronunciation.

This illustrates the value of practicing what
could be called situational phonetics, or the
when-in-Rome-approach to pronunciation. It
would be folly to use the French pronunciation

when asking a clerk in a beer and wine store for a bottle of Bollinger or Piper Heidsick champagne. A waiter in Reims might find the American pronunciations equally incomprehensible.

Haute as in Oat was conceived to be practical and useful rather than encyclopedic. To that end, names and terms on menus and wine lists that are seldom or never mispronounced aren't included. Some of the ones that are may come as surprises.

Acknowledgements

WANTED: chef-linguist with mastery of cuisines and languages of France, Germany and Italy, able to discourse authoritatively on food and wines in impeccable English.

Had I, in searching for the ideal consultant, run such an ad in European and American periodicals, I suspect my chances of discovering someone with those awesome credentials would have been negligible at best. It's against those odds I measure my good fortune in knowing Charity deVecq Suczek, whose help and counsel were invaluable to me in preparing this guide.

Born in Imperial Vienna into a family of French ancestry, Mrs. Suczek is a graduate of Oxford University (Romance Languages) and Le Cordon Bleu in Paris. After apprenticing with leading chefs in Europe and the Orient, she opened Le Petit Corden Bleu—a finishing school for cooks in Grosse Pointe, Michigan. She is fluent in seven languages.

I'm indebted to the several linguists who tape recorded the pronunciations transcribed herein: Christine Filipoz, Jelena Franklin, Professor Marco Nobili and Charity Suczek.

Liesel Geiger, Marion Main and Denis Vajs provided valuable research assistance. London Restaurateur Luigi Tosi, Professor Monique Wagner, and translators Barbara Leitner and Vittorio Re fastidiously checked for and corrected errors in the text.

Molly Swart of the French Trade Commission and Sommelier Madeline Triffon of the London Chop House in Detroit were most helpful in furnishing resource material and in identifying information sources.

Ann Westcott devised a way to create the alpha indexes by computer, and cheerfully undertook the laborious task of inputting the entries.

As PC operator, data-flow manager and archivist, my wife, Janet, deserves most of the credit for the fact that "Haute as in Oat" appeared in this decade.

Last to be recognized but foremost in the scheme of things is my editor, Charles Lean. The idea for the book emerged from our discussions, and I'm grateful for his sustained enthusiasm, encouragement and support.

How to Use the Guide

- Pronunciations appear in parenthesis.
- Boldface type indicates emphasis.
- Common English words are used whenever possible to indicate how a word or a part of a word should be pronounced.

  If a combination of letters spells a common English word (like *me, knee* or *re,* for examples) it's the sound of that word that's called for. Made-up words (like *lawm* and *moosh*) should be sounded out instinctively.

- A zh indicates that the sound of the French je (as in *je vous aime*) is called for.

- This guide is designed both for browsing and reference. If you want to find the pronunciation of a particular word you've seen on a menu or wine list, turn to the appropriate index (French, German or Italian) where all the names or terms are listed alphabetically. If the name in question is *sogliola,* for instance, the Italian index will refer you to a page in Fish, Shellfish and Mollusks. There you'll find that it means sole and is pronounced **sole**-yole-a.

  The guide's mission is to provide pronunciations. But, translations are offered for the basic ingredients of menu entries, on the principle that the reader who is allergic to shellfish or craves wild game should be advised that *homard* is lobster in French and *selvaggina* is Italian for venison. However, the guide leaves to chefs and cookbooks the job of defining sauces and styles of preparation.

FRENCH

Food and Wine

Pronunciation Tips

The French "u" and "n" sound defiantly un-American. Mastering them is guaranteed to upgrade your pronunciations from tourist class.

The French pronounce "u" in words they way we do when we recite the alphabet. *Fumet,* for instance, is pronounced "few-may," but that's one of the rare cases where the proper value of the "u" is easy to indicate. With a word like *duxelles* the guide settles for "duke-sell" rather than risk confusing the reader with a complicated analogue like "dyuke-sell." For best results just add the missing ingredient when you come across a "u."

The "n" in French is seldom pronounced unless it starts a word or is doubled. Usually it's just a nasal sound dictated by the preceding vowel, and in all such cases in this guide, the "n" is italicised for easy recognition. In the pronunciations e*n* crops up dozens of times and the sound it calls for is what you hear when you try to say "en" holding your mouth wide open. Likewise, when you see a*n* or o*n* the sounds called for are what you produce when you try to say "an" or "on" with your mouth open.

Another quirk to be aware of is that "m" has the same value as a nasal "n" in many words. So you'll often find an "m" and its preceding vowel rendered in the pronunciations as e*n,* a*n* or o*n.*

When accented vowels are capitalized the French usually dispense with the accent signs. As an aid to word recognition this guide retains them.

Les Termes Culinaires/Culinary Terms

(lay-tairm cue-lee-**nayr**)

Aigre/sour
  (**egg**-gruh)

Ailerons/wings (poultry)
  (ay-luh-ro*n*)

Amer/bitter
  (ah-**mare**)

Andouille/chitterling sausage
  (a*n*-do-**ee**)

Arêtes, sans/boneless (fish)
  (sa*nz*-ah-**ret**)

Attereau/skewer
  (ah-tuh-**row**)

Bardé/wrapped in fat, as for a roast
  (bar-**day**)

Beurre/butter
  (burr)

Beurre manié/butter-flour paste
  (burr-man-**yay**)

Bien cuit/well done
  (be-e*n* **kwee**)

Broche, à la/to cook on a skewer
  (ah lah **brawsh**)

Café noir/black coffee
  (cah-fay nwar)

Casse-croute/snack
  (cass-**croot**)

Cassoulet/stew of meat and beans
  (**cassoo**-lay)

Chaud/hot
(show)

Chipolata/little pork sausage
(she-poh-lah-**tah**)

Choucroute/sauerkraut
(**shoe**-croot)

Concassé/coarsely chopped
(con-cass-**say**)

Confit/preserved, such as fruits in sugar, goose in fat
(con-**fee**)

Coquille, en/in the shell
(on co-**key**)

Court bouillon/flavored poaching liquid
(coor boo-yon)

Cru/raw
(crew)

Darne/slice of fish
(darn)

Daube/braised meat
(doe-b)

Desossé/boned
(day-zossay)

Diable, à la/deviled; with mustard coating
(ah lah dee-**ahb**-luh)

Duxelles/diced cooked mushrooms
(duke-**sell**)

Émincé/sliced, usually meat
(ay-men-**say**)

Épicé/spicy
(ay-pea-**say**)

Estragon/tarragon
(ess-trah-**gon**)

Farci/stuffed
(far-**see**)

Fines herbes/herb mixture
(feenz **airb**)

Flan/custard tart
(fla*n*)

Fond/bottom
(fo*n*)

Froid/cold
(frwah)

Fumet/fish or vegetable stock
(few-**may**)

Garni/garnished
(gar-**nee**)

Gelée, en/in aspic
(*an* zhuh-**lay**)

Glacé/chilled or glazed
(gla-**say**)

Gras/fat
(grah)

Haché/finely chopped or ground
(a-**shay**)

Jardinière/diced vegetables
(zhar-deen-**yair**)

Julienne/cut into matchstick size
(zhool-**yen**)

Jus, au/with nautral juice
(oh-**zhew**)

Lait, au/with milk
(oh-**lay**)

Lardé/meat inserted with fat strips
(lar-**day**)

Macédoine/mixed diced fruits or vegetables
(mass-ay-**dwan**)

Macéré/steeped or soaked in special flavors
(mah-say-**ray**)

Mouillé/moistened
  (moo-**yay**)

Mousse/light and airy dish
  (moose)

Mousseux/foamy
  (moose-**uh**)

Naturel, au/plain
  (oh-na-tew-**rell**)

Noisette/nut brown as for browned butter
  (nwah **zet**)

Nouilles/noodles
  (**noo**-yuh)

Os/bone
  (os)

Panaché/mixed, usually vegetables
  (pah-nah-**shay**)

Pané/coated with crumbs
  (pah-**nay**)

Papillote, en/baked in parchment
  (*an* pappy-**yot**)

Parfait/a smooth frozen cream
  (par-**fay**)

Pelé/peeled
  (puh-**lay**)

Piquante/tart, biting
  (pea-**cant**)

Quenelles/fish or meat dumplings
  (cuh-**nell**)

Ragoût/a stew
  (rah-**goo**)

Rillettes/cooked shredded pork
  (ree-**yet**)

Rôti/roast
  (roe-**tee**)

Roux/butter and flower paste
(roo)

Salmis/a ragout usually of game birds
(sal-**me**)

Salpicon/sauced tidbits
(sal-pea-**co**n)

Saupoudré/sprinkled as with grated cheese
(so-poo-**dray**)

Tourte/covered meat pie, or open-faced tart
(tourt)

Vol-au-vent/puff pastry container
(vul-oh-**va**n)

Les Méthodes Culinaires/
Cooking Methods
(lay may-tuhd cue-lee-**nayr**)

Blanchi/blanched
(bla*n*-**she**)

Bouilli/boiled
(boo-**yee**)

Braisé/braised
(bray-**zay**)

Brûlé/flamed
(brew-**lay**)

Daube/stew
(doe-b)

Étuvée, à l'/slow cooked
(ah lay tue-**vay**)

Flambé/flamed
(fla*n*-bay)

Four, au/in the oven; baked
(oh **foor**)

Fricassée/a white stew
(freak-as**say**)

Frit/fried
(free)

Frites, les/French fries
(lay **freet**)

Gratiné/browned on top
(grah-tee-**nay**)

Grillé/grilled
(gree-**yay**)

Mijoté/slowly simmered
(me-zho-**tay**)

Nage, à la/served in its broth
  (ah lah **nazh**)

Poché/poached
  (poe-**shay**)

Rissolé/browned in a frying pan
  (ree-soh-**lay**)

Rôti/roast
  (roh-**tee**)

Sauté/quick fried
  (soh-**tay**)

Vapeur, à la/steamed
  (ah lah vah-**purr**)

Les Sauces/Sauces

(lay-sohss)

Aioli
(eye-oh-**lee**)

Albert
(al-**bear**)

Allemande
(ah-luh-**mand**)

Américaine
(ah-mair-ee-**ken**)

Andalouse
(*an*-da-lose)

Aurore
(oh-**roar**)

Banquière
(ba*n*-kyair)

Bâtarde
(bah-**tard**)

Béarnaise
(bay-ar**nez**)

Beauharnais
(bo-are-**neh**)

Béchamel
(bay-shah-**mell**)

Bercy
(bare-**see**)

Beurre blanc
(burr bla*n*)

Beurre noir
(burr nwar)

Bigarade
(big-ar-**ad**)

Bonnefoy
(bun-fwah)

Bontemps
(bo*n*-ta*n*)

Bordelaise
(bore-duh-**lez**)

Bourguignonne
(boor-**geen**-yon)

Cardinal
(car-dee-**nahl**)

Chambertin
(sha*n*-bare-ta*n*)

Chambord
(sha*n*-**bore**)

Chapelure
(shap-uh-lure)

Charcutière
(shar-cue-**tyair**)

Chasseur
(shah-**sir**)

Chaud-froid
(show-frwah)

Chivry
(she-**vree**)

Choron
(sho-**ro*n***)

Cingalaise
(se*n*-ga-lez)

Colbert
(coll-**bare**)

Collioure
(coll-your)

Cressonnière
(cresson-**yare**)

Demi-glace
(duh-me-glass)

Diane
(dee-**ann**)

Dijonnaise
(deezhon-**nez**)

Duxelles
(duke-sell)

Écossaise
(echo-says)

Financière
(fin-*an*-see-**air**)

Genevoise
(zhen-vwaahz)

Genoise
(zhen-**waahz**)

Gribiche
(gree-**beesh**)

Hachée
(a-**shay**)

Hollandaise
(all-la*n*-**dez**)

Ivoire
(eve-oh-**are**)

Joinville
(zhwe*n*-veal)

Maître d' hotel
(metruh doe-tell)

Marinière
(marin-**yair**)

Matelote
(mah-tuh-**lot**)

Mayonnaise
(mah-yon-**nez**)

Mignonette
(minion-**et**)

Mornay
(more-**nay**)

Mousquetaire
(moose-cuh-**tair**)

Mousseline
(moose-uh-**leen**)

Mousseuse
(moose-ooze)

Nantaise
(na*n*-**tez**)

Nantua
(na*n*-tue-**ah**)

Napolitaine
(na-poly-**ten**)

Paloise
(pall-**wahz**)

Parisienne
(pah-reez-**yen**)

Périgourdine
(perry-goor-**deen**)

Perigueux
(perry-**guh**)

Piquante
(pick-**a*n*t**)

Piemontaise
(pee-yay-mo*n*tez)

Polonaise
(polo-nez)

Princesse
(pre*n*-**sess**)

Printanière
(pre*n*-tan-**yair**)

Provençal
(pro-va*n*-**sal**)

Ravigote
(rah-vee-**got**)

Régence
(ray-**zha*n*ss**)

Rémoulade
(raymoo-**lad**)

Riche
(**reesh**)

Rouennaise
(roo-an-**nez**)

Sardalaise
(sar-da-**lez**)

Velouté
(vuh-loo-**tay**)

Veneur
(ven-**ur**)

Véon
(vay-o*n*)

Verdurette
(vair-du**ret**)

Villeroy
(veal-**rwah**)

Vinaigrette
(vee-nay-**gret**)

Vincent
(ve*n*-**sa*n***)

Les noms et les façons de préparation/Names and styles of preparation

(lay nom ay lay fasso*n* duh pray-par-ass-**syo*n***)

Agenaise, à l'
  (ah lah-zhuh-**nez**)

Albigeoise, à l'
  (ah lal-bee-**zhwahs**)

Algérienne, à l'
  (ah lal-zhay-ree-**en**)

Alsacienne, à l'
  (ah lal-zass-**yen**)

Ambassadrice, à l'
  (ah la*n*bassa-**dreese**)

Ancienne, à l'
  (ah la*n*s-**yen**)

Anglaise, à l'
  (ah la*n*-**glez**)

Antiboise, à l'
  (ah la*n*ty-**bwahz**)

Arlésienne, à l'
  (ah lar-laze-**yen**)

Argenteuil
  (are-zha*n*-**toy**)

Armenonville
  (are-muh-no*n*-**veal**)

Aromates, aux
  (oh zarrow-**mat**)

Attereaux, aux
  (oh zatter-**oh**)

17

Augier
(oh-zhee-**ay**)

Bachaumont
(bash-oh-**mo***n*)

Bamboche
(ba*n*-**bosh**)

Barquettes
(bar-**ket**)

Basilic
(bah-zee-**leek**)

Bayonnaise
(bay-on-**nez**)

Béatrix
(bay-a-**treece**)

Beignets
(bane-**yay**)

Belle-Hélène
(bell ay-**len**)

Bellevoilloise
(bell-vwall-wahz)

Berrichonne
(berry-**shon**)

Biarrote
(be-a-**rot**)

Boivin
(bwah-ve*n*)

Bonne femme
(bun-**fam**)

Bonvalet
(bo*n*-vall**ay**)

Boulangère
(boo-la*n*-**zhair**)

Bouchère
(boo-**share**)

Bourgeoise
  (boor-**zhwahz**)

Bretonne
  (breh-**tawn**)

Brillat-Savarin
  (bree-yah sa-vah-re*n*)

Brossard
  (bro-**sar**)

Bruxelloise
  (brew-sell-**wahz**)

Campagne
  (ca*n*-**pan**-yuh)

Canalaise
  (cana-**lez**)

Cancalaise
  (ca*n*-ca-**lez**)

Carignan
  (car-ee-**nya*n***)

Carmélite
  (carmay-**leet**)

Carnavalet
  (carnah-vall**ay**)

Cassolettes
  (caso-**let**)

Célestine
  (say-less-**teen**)

Chablisienne
  (shab-leez-**yen**)

Champvallon
  (sha*n*-va-**lo*n***)

Châtelaine
  (shat-**len**)

Chauchat
  (show-**shah**)

Chevalière
  (sheval-**yare**)

Chevreuil
  (shuh-**vroy**)

Chevreuse
  (shuh-**vruse**)

Chivry
  (she-**vree**)

Choisy
  (shwah-**zee**)

Coq au vin
  (cuck oh ve*n*)

Cordon bleu
  (core-do*n*-**bluh**)

Créole
  (cray-**ole**)

Cressonière
  (cresson-**yare**)

Crapaudine
  (crap-oh-**deen**)

Cussy
  (cue-**see**)

Custine
  (cue-**steen**)

Daumont
  (doe-**mo*n***)

Dauphine
  (doe-**feen**)

Diablotins
  (dee-ablo-**te*n***)

Dieppoise
  (dee-ep-**wahz**)

Demi-deuil
  (duh-me-**doy**)

Dreux
(drew)

Duroc
(dew-**rock**)

Échelle
(ay-**shell**)

Écarlate
(ay-car-**lot**)

Écossaise
(ay-co-**says**)

Émincés
(ay-me*n*-say)

Favart
(fa-**var**)

Fécampoise
(fay-ca*n*-**pwahz)**

Fédora
(fay-dor**a**)

Fermière
(fur-me-**air**)

Flamande
(flam-**a*n*d**)

Forestière
(for-est-**yair**)

Français
(fra*n*-**say**)

Gauloise
(goal-**wahz**)

Hongroise
(o*n*-**grwahz**)

Hôtelière
(otel-**yare**)

Indienne, à l'
(ah le*n*-**dyen**)

Jacques
(zhock)

Lambertye
(lam-bear-**tee**)

Languedocienne
(la*n*-guh-doss-**yen**)

Leverrier
(luh-vair-yay)

Limousine
(lee-moo-**zeen**)

Livonienne
(lee-vone-**yen**)

Loraine
(lo-**ren**)

Lucullus
(**lew**-cool-oo*ss*)

Lyonnaise
(leo-**nez**)

Macédoine
(mass-ay-**dwan**)

Madrilène
(mad-ree-**len**)

Maintenon
(me*n*-tuh-**no***n*)

Maraîchere
(marray-**share**)

Maréchale
(mar-ay-**shall**)

Marivaux
(marry-**vo**)

Matignon
(mah-tee-nyo*n*)

Ménagère
(may-nah-**zhair**)

Meunière
  (muh-**nyair**)

Meurette
  (mur-**et**)

Milanaise
  (me-la-**nez**)

Mireille
  (me-**ray**)

Mirepoix
  mere-**pwah**)

Monselet
  (mo*n*-suh-**lay**)

Montbry
  (mo*n*-**bree**)

Montpensier
  (mo*n*-pan-see-**yay**)

Montreuil
  (mo*n*-**troy**)

Montrouge
  (mo*n*-**roozh**)

Nichette
  (neesh-et)

Niçoise
  (niece-**wahz**)

Normande
  (nor-**ma*n*d**)

Occitane, à l'
  (ah-loxy-**tan**)

Orly
  (or-**lee**)

Panetière
  (pan-uh-**tyair**)

Parisienne
  (pareez-**yen**)

Parmentier
(par-ma*n*-**tyay**)

Paysanne
(payee-**zan**)

Pépita
(pay-pee-**tah**)

Périgord
(perry-**gore**)

Périgueux
(perry-**guh**)

Petit-duc
(ptee **duke**)

Pistache
(pee-**stash**)

Portefeuille
(port-**foy**)

Poitevine
(pwah-tuh-**veen**)

Portugaise
(por-tue-**gez**)

Reine-Jeanne
(ren-**zhan**)

Renière
(ruh-**nyair**)

Richelieu
(reesh-ul-**yuh**)

Rouennaise
(roo-ah-**nez**)

Rougail
(roo-**guy**)

Rouille
(**roo**-yuh)

Russe
(rewss)

Saint-Germain
(se*n*-zhair-**me***n*)

Saint-Hubert
(se*n*-tue-**bare**)

Salpicon
(sal-pee-**co***n*)

Sardalaise
(sar-da-**lez**)

Sévigné
(say-vee-**nyay**)

Soissonnaise
(swah-sun-**nez**)

Soubise
(soo-**beez**)

Strasbourgeoise
(strass-boor-**zhwahz**)

Talleyrand
(tallay-ra*n*)

Toulouse
(to-**lose**)

Turque
(tewrk)

Tyrolienne
(tea-roll-**yen**)

Valencienne
(val-a*n*ce-**yen**)

Vanneau
(van-**no**)

Vauclusienne
(vo-clue-zyen)

Vénitienne
(vay-nee-**syen**)

Verdurière
(vair-dur-**yair**)

Véron
  (vay-**ron**)

Viennoise
  (veen-**nwahz**)

Viveur
  (vee-**vurr**)

Hors-d'oeuvre/Appetizers

(or **dove**-ruh)

Artichauts Juan-les-pins
  (arty-show zhua*n*-lay-pe*n*)

Beignets
  (bane-yay)

Boulettes de volaille
  (boolet duh vo-**lye**)

Canapés Jeannette
  (can-a-pay zhah-net)

  Marquis à la margery
    (mar-**key** a la mar-zhuh-**re**)

  Micheline
    (meesh-lean)

  Rochelaise
    (rosh-lez)

Céleriac Rémoulade
  (sell-air-yak ray-moo-**lad**)

Cigarettes au foie gras
  (oh fwah grah)

Cigarettes de Bayonne
  (see-ga-**ret** duh bah-yon)

Croûtes au fromage gratinée
  (croot oh fro-mazh gra-teen-**ay**)

Croûtes pour entrées mixés
  (croot poor a*n*tray meek-say)

Foie gras en brioche
  (**fwah** grah a*n* bree-**osh**)

Pâté de foie gras
  (**pah**-tay duh fwah grah)

Profiteroles
(pro-**feet**-uh-roll)

Quiche
(keesh)

Les Pains/Breads

(lay pen)

Brioche
  (bree-**yohsh**)

Croissants
  (krwah-sa*n*)

Natte
  (naht)

Pain azyme
  (pe*n* **ah** zeem)

Pain de ménage
  (pe*n* duh may-nazh)

Pain Français en rouleau
  (pe*n* **fra***n*-say **a***n* roo-**lo**)

Petits pain au lait
  (ptee **pe***n* oh-**lay**)

Petits pain aux oeufs
  (ptee **pe***n* oh **zuh**)

Les Potages/Soups
(lay po-tazh)

Bijane
  (be-**zhan**)

Bouillabaisse
  (boo-ya-**bess**)

Bourride
  (boor-**reed**)

Chaud rée de fouras
  (show ray duh foo**ra**)

Consommé
  (con-so-**may**)

Consommé simple de volaille
  (senpl duh vo-**lie**)

Court bouillon au vinaigre
  (coor boo-yon oh vee-**nay**gruh)

Crécy
  (cray-**see**)

Pipérade
  (pea**pay**-rad)

Pistou
  (pea-**stew**)

Pot-au-feu
  (pot oh **fuh**)

Vichyssoise
  (veeshy-swahz)

Viandes et Gibiers/
Meat and Game

(vee-a*n*d ay zheeb-**yay**)

Agneau/lamb
  (an-**yo**)

Boeuf/beef
  (buff)*

Chèvre/goat
  (**shev**-ruh)

Chevreuil/roe-deer or roe-buck
  (shev-**roy**)

Cochon de lait/suckling pig
  (co-sho*n* duh **lay**)

Gibier/wild game
  (zheeb-**yay**)

Jambon/ham
  (zha*n*-**bo***n*)

Jambon frais/fresh pork leg; fresh ham
  (zha*n*-bo*n*-**fray**)

Lapereau/young rabbit
  (lah-**pro**)

Lapin/rabbit
  (la-**pe***n*)

Lièvre/wild hare
  (**lee-ev**-ruh)

Marcassin/young wild boar
  (mar-cass-**se***n*)

Mouton/mutton
  (moo-**to***n*)

*The "u" in buff is a rough approximation of the vowel sound in boeuf. The
  "u" in turf is much closer.

Sanglier/wild boar
  (sa*n*-glee-**yay**)

Veau/veal
  (vo)

Venaison/venison
  (vuh-nay-**zo***n*)

Coupes de viandes/Meat cuts

(coop-duh-vee-**and**)

Aiguillette/part of beef rump
　(ay-gwee-**yet**)

Aloyau/whole bone-in loin
　(ah-low-**yo**)

Baron d'agneau/whole hind quarter of lamb
　(bah-ron danyo)

Baron de boeuf/double bone-in whole loin
　(bah-ron duh **buff**)*

Carré/rack—whole rib chop section
　(car-**ray**)

Cervelles/brains
　(sir-**vel**)

Châteaubriand/steak from heart of tenderloin
　(sha-toe-bree-**yan**)

Contre-filet/top loin strip steak
　(con-truh-fee-**lay**)

Coeur/heart
　(cur)

Côte/pork chop
　(coat)

Côtelette/lamb or veal chop
　(co-**tlet**)

Culotte/rump section of beef
　(cue-**lot**)

Entrecôte/rib steak
　(antruh-coat)

Escalope/thin slices of meat
　(ess-cal-**lop**)

*See footnote page 33.

Faux-filet/top loin strip steak
  (foh-fee-**lay**)

Filet/tenderloin
  (fee-**lay**)

Filet mignon/steaks from small end of
  tenderloin
  (fee-lay me-**nyo***n*)

Foie/liver
  (fwah)

Gigot/leg, as in leg of lamb
  (zhee-**go**)

Gras-double/thickest part of the tripe
  (grah-**doob**-luh)

Jambonneau/small end of the shank, usually
  boneless
  (zha*n*-bun-**no**)

Jarret/shank
  (zhar-**ray**)

Langue/tongue
  (**la***n*-guh)

Longe/bone-in whole loin of pork or veal
  (lo*n*zh)

Médallions/small boneless rounds of tender
  meat
  (may-dye-**yo***n*)

Noisettes/smaller than médallions
  (nwah-**zet**)

Onglet/beef along backbone
  (o*n*-**glay**)

Paleron/chuck shoulder, blade portion
  (pal-**ro***n*)

Paupiette/thin slices of meat, rolled
  (poh-pea-**yet**)

Pied/foot
  (pea-**yay**)

Plat de côtes/beef back ribs
  (plah duh **coat**)

Poitrine/brisket
  (pwah-**treen**)

Quasi/sirloin section
  (kah-**zee**)

Queue/tail
  (kuh)

Rognon/kidney
  (ron-nyo*n*)

Ris/sweetbreads
  (ree)

Selle/saddle
  (sell)

Tendrons/breast rib-ends
  (ta*n*-dro*n*)

Tournedos/middle size tenderloin steaks
  (tour-neh-**doe**)

Tripes/tripe
  (treep)

Volaille/Fowl

(voh-**lie**)

Bécasse/woodcock
  (bay-**cass**)

Caille/quail
  (**cah**-yuh)

Canard/duck
  (can-**ar**)

Caneton/duckling
  (can-eh **ton**)

Chapon/capon
  (shah-**pon**)

Coq/rooster
  (cuck)

Dindon/turkey
  (den-**don**)

Dindonneau/young turkey
  (den-don-**no**)

Faisan/pheasant
  (fez-**an**)

Grive/thrush
  (grieve)

Grouse/grouse
  (grooze)

Oie/goose
  (wah)

Perdreau/partridge
  (pair-**droh**)

Pigeon/pigeon
  (pea-**zhon**)

Pintade/guinea hen
  (pe*n*-**tad**)

Poularde/roasting chicken
  (poo-**lard**)

Poule/stewing hen
  (pull)

Poulet/young chicken, a fryer
  (poo-**lay**)

Poussin/small 1-lb. chicken
  (poo-se*n*)

Poissons, Crustacés et Mollusques/Fish, Shellfish and Mollusks

(pwahs-so*n*, crew-stah-**say** ay mole-**oos**kuh)

Alose/shad
  (ah-**lows**)

Anchois/anchovy
  (o*n*-**shwah**)

Anguille/eel
  (o*n*-gee (as in geek))

Barbue/brill
  (bar-**bew**)

Bars/sea bass
  (bar)

Brochet/pike
  (bro-**shay**)

Cabillaud/cod
  (cah-be-**yoh**)

Calmar/squid
  (calmar)

Carrelet/plaice
  (car-uh-**lay**)

Congre/sea eel, conger eel
  (**con**-gruh)

Coquilles St.Jacques/scallops
  (co-key se*n*-**zhock**)

Crabe/crab
  (crob)

Crevette/shrimp
  (cruh-**vet**)

Crevette rouge/prawns
  (cruh-**vet** roozh)

Daurade/sea-bream; porgy
  (doe-**rad**)

Écrevisse/crawfish
  (ay-cruh-**veess**)

Églefin/haddock
  (ay-gluh-**fe***n*)

Éperlan/smelt
  (epper-**la***n*)

Escargot/snail
  (ess-car-**go**)

Flet/flounder
  (fleh)

Goujon/gudgeon; white-bait
  (goo-**zho***n*)

Grenouille/frog
  (gruh-**new**-yuh)

Homard/lobster
  (oh-**mar**)

Huître/oyster
  (**we**-truh)

Langoustine/Norway lobster; Dublin Bay
  prawn
  (la*n*-goose-**teen**)

Langouste/spiny lobster
  (la*n*-**goost**)

Lotte/monkfish
  (lot)

Loup de mer/sea bass
  (loo-duh-**mare**)

Macquereau/mackerel
  (mack-uh-**roe**)

Morue/salt cod
  (mo-**rew**)

Moule/mussel
(mool)

Oursin/sea urchin
(oor-**sen**)

Palourde/clam
(pah-**loord**)

Perche/perch
(**pairsh**)

Poulpe/octopus
(**pool**-p)

Raie/skate
(ray)

Rouget/red mullet
(roo-**zhay**)

Sardines/sardine
(sahr-**deen**)

Saumon/salmon
(so-**mon**)

Sole/sole
(soul)

Thon/tuna
(ton)

Truite/trout
(tre-**weet**)

Turbot/turbot
(tour-bo)

Manières d'apprêter les oeufs/
Egg Cooking Methods

(man-yair dah-preh-tay lay **zuh**)

Pronunciation note: The sound of the vowels in *oeuf,* the French word for egg, isn't used in English. The closest we come is the "u" in turf. If you say urf, then repeat it without the "r", you've pretty well got it. The plural, oeufs, is trickier because both the "f" and the "s" are silent. So, just the "u" sound in urf is called for. When oeufs is preceded by the article *les* (the), the "s" in *les* is pronounced and bonds with *oeufs*—producing sounds that can best be rendered as "lay-**zuh**."

les oeufs brouillés/scrambled eggs
   (lay-**zuh** broo-**yea**)

   à la coque/soft boiled eggs
      (ah lah **cock**)

---

   en cocotte/eggs in ramekins
      (*an* co-cot)

---

   dur/hard-boiled eggs
      (dewr)

---

   frits/French fried eggs
      (freet)

---

   miroir/broiled eggs
      (mere-**wahr**)

---

   sur le plat/shirred eggs
      (sewr-luh-**plah**)

---

   pochés/poached eggs
      (poe-**shay**)

   à la poêle/American-style fried eggs
      (ah lah **pwal**)

Legumes/Vegetables (and fungi)
(*lay*-**gyoom**)

Ail/garlic
  (eye)

Artichaut/artichoke
  (arty-**show**)

Asperge/asparagus
  (ah-**spairzh**)

Betterave/beets
  (bet-**trahv**)

Bruxelles/brussel sprouts
  (brew-**sell**)

Cardon/cardoon
  (car-**don**)

Carrotes/carrots
  (car-rot)

Céleris/celery
  (say-luh-**ree**)

Cèpes/variety of mushroom
  (sep)

Champignons/mushrooms
  (shan-**pee**-**nyon**)

Châtaigne d'eau/water chestnut
  (shat-ain-yuh **doe**)

Chou/cabbage
  (shoe)

Chou-fleur/cauliflower
  (shoe-**flerr**)

Ciboulette/chive
  (see-boo-**let**)

Concombre/cucumber
(con-conbruh)

Cornichon/gherkin
(corny-shon)

Courgettes/zucchini
(coor-**zhet**)

Courge/pumpkin
(coorzh)

Cresson/watercress
(cres-son)

Échalote/shallot
ay-shah-**lot**)

Endive/endive
(an-deev)

Épinards/spinach
(ay-pee-**nar**)

Féveroles/field beans
(fay-ver-**ohl**)

Flageolets/green kidney beans
(flah-zho-**lay**)

Haricot verts/green beans
(arry-**co** vair)

Igname/yam
(een-yam)

Laitue/lettuce
(lay-**tyew**)

Lentille/lentil
(lan-**tee**)

Navets/turnips
(nah-**veh**)

Oignons/onions
(o-nyon)

Orge/barley
(orzh)

Oseille/sorrel
  (oh-zay)

Panais/parsnip
  (pah-**nay**)

Pâtisson/squash
  (patty-so*n*)

Persil/parsley
  (pair-**see**)

Piments/red peppers
  (pee**ma***n*)

Piments doux/sweet pepper
  (peema*n*-**do**)

Pommes de terre/potatoes
  (pum duh tare)

Pois/peas
  (pwah)

Poireau/leeks
  (pwah-**roe**)

Radis/radishes
  (rah-**dee**)

Raifort/horseradish
  (ray-**for**)

Tomate/tomato
  (toe-**mat**)

Truffe/truffles
  (troof)

Entremets et leurs apprêts/
Dessert Basics

(*an*-truh-may ay luhr-zah **preh**)

Amande/almond
  (ah-**mand**)

Bavarois/Bavarian cream
  (bah-var-**wah**)

Beignet/batter-fried fruit
  (bay-**nyay**)

Bombe/molded ice creams
  (bo*n*b)

Cannelle/cinnamon
  (can-**nel**)

Caramel/caramel
  (cah-rah-**mel**)

Charlotte/cylindrical mold
  (shar-**lot**)

Charlotte de pommes/molded apple dessert
  (shar-lot duh **pum**)

Chocolat/chocolate
  (shocko-**lah**)

Clafoutis/fruit custard tart
  (clah-foo-**tee**)

Compote/stewed fruits
  (co*n*-**pot**)

Confiture/fruit preserves
  (co*n*-fee-**ture**)

Crème/cream, custard
  (crem)

      anglaise/custard sauce
  (a*n*-**glez**)

Crème au beurre/butter-cream
  (oh-**burr**)

      Chantilly/softly whipped cream
        (shan-**tee**-yee)

      fleurette/American-style heavy cream
        (flur-**rett**)

      fraîche/French slightly sour heavy
      cream
        (**fresh**)

      pâtissière/custard filling
        (pah-tee-**syair**)

      renversée au caramel/molded
      caramel custard
        (ran-ver-**say** oh cah-rah-**mel**)

Crêpe/thin pancake
  (crep)

Gelée/jelly
  (zhuh-**lay**)

Girofle/clove
  (zhee-**rofe**-luh)

Glace/ice cream
  (glass)

Macis/mace
  (mas-**see**)

Madeleine/shell-shaped cookie
  (mad-**len**)

Marmelade/marmelade
  (mar-muh-**lad**)

Meringue/meringue
  (muh-**reng**)

Miel/honey
  (mee-**yel**)

Moka/coffee-chocolate flavor
  (moh-**kah**)

Mont-blanc/puréed chestnut dessert
(mon-**blan**)

Mousse au chocolat/chocolate mousse
(moose oh shocko-**lah**)

Noisette/hazelnut
(nwah-**zet**)

Noix/walnut
(nwah)

Omelette soufflé/soufléed omelet
(om-let soo-**flay**)

Parfait/a silky ice cream
(par-**fay**)

Pâte d'amande/marzipan
paht da-ma*n*d)

Pistache/pistachio
(peas-**tash**)

Pralin/carmelized ground nuts
(prah-**len**)

Riz à l'impératrice/fancy cold rice custard
(ree ah le*n*-pair-ah-**treess**)

Sabayon/warm foamy egg sauce
(sah-bah-**yon**)

Sirop/syrup
(see-**roh**)

Sorbet/sherbet
(sore-**bay**)

Sucre glace/confectioners sugar
(sue-kruh glass)

Tarte/tart
(tart)

Tartelette/small tart
(tart-uh-**let**)

Timbale/molded custard
(te*n*-**bal**)

Torte/cake
  (tort)

Vanille/vanilla
  (va-**knee**)

Pâtisserie/Cake and Pastry Basics

(pah-tees-sir**ee**)

Allumette/finger-shaped pastries
  (ah-loo-**met**)

Baba/small rum cake
  (bah-**bah**)

Biscuit/sponge cake
  (bee-**skwee**)

Biscuits à la cuiller/ladyfingers
  (be-**skwee** ah lah kwee-**yair**)

Bonbon/small candy
  bo*n*-**bo***n*)

Chausson/covered tart
  (show-**so***n*)

Choux à la créme/round cream puff
  (shoe ah la craym)

Confiserie/confectionery, preserves
  (co*n*-fee-zuh-**re**)

Crème au beurre/butter-cream
  (crem oh **burr**)

Croûte/crust
  (kroot)

Éclair/finger-shaped cream puff
  (ay-**clair**)

Feuilletage/puff pastry dough
  (fuh-yuh-**tazh**)

Fondant/fondant
  (fo*n*-**da***n*)

Galette/a round pastry
  (gah-**let**)

Gâteau/cake
(ga-**toe**)

Gaufre/waffle
(**go**-fruh)

Langues-de-chat/tongue-shaped sugar
cookies
(la*n*g-duh-**shah**)

Levure chimique/baking powder
(luh-vure she-**meek**)

Levure de boulanger/baker's yeast
(luh-vure duh boo-la*n*-**zhay**)

Macaron/macaroon
(mah-cah-**ro*n***)

Pain de Gênes/almond cake
(pe*n* duh **zhen**)

Pâte/pastry dough
(paht)

   à choux/cream puff pastry
   (ah **shoe**)

   à frire/batter for deep frying
   (ah **freer**)

   brisée/pie crust dough
   (bree-**zay**)

   feuilleté/French puff pastry dough
   (fuh-yuh-**tay**)

Petits fours/individual cakes
(ptee-**foor**)

Sablés/sugar cookies
(saw-**blay**)

Savarin/round rum cake with central hole
(saw-vah-re*n*)

Tuiles/tile shaped cookies
(tweel)

Fruit/Fruit
(frwee)

Abricot/apricot
  (ah-bree-**coh**)

Ananas/pineapple
  (an-nah-**nahs**)

Banane/banana
  (ban-**nan**)

Baie/berry
  (bay)

Canneberge/cranberry
  (can-berzh)

Cassis/black currant
  (ca-**see**)

Cerise/cherry
  (sreez)

Citron/lemon
  (see-**tro***n*)

Coing/quince
  (**kew**n)

Figues/figs
  (feeg)

Fraise/strawberry
  (frez)

Framboise/raspberry
  (fra*n*-bwahz)

Grain de raisin/grape
  (gre*n* duh ray-**ze***n*)

Groseille/red currant
  (grow-**zay**)

Limettes/limes
  (lee**met**)

Mandarine/tangerine
  (man-da-**reen**)

Mangue/mango
  (ma*n*-guh)

Melon/melon
  (muh-**lo***n*)

Orange/orange
  (or-a*n*zh)

Pamplemousse/grapefruit
  (pa*n*-pluh-moose)

Pêche/peach
  (pesh)

Poire/pear
  (pwahr)

Pomme/apple
  (pum)

Prune/plum
  (prewn)

Pruneau/dried prune
  (prew-**noh**)

Raisin/raisin
  (ray-**ze***n*)

Les Fromages/Cheeses

(lay froh-mazh)

Banon
  (bah-non)

Beaufort
  (bo-for)

Beaumont
  (bo-mon)

Belle-Bressane
  (bel bress-sahn)

Bleu d'Auvergne
  (bluh doe-vare-nyuh)

Bleu des Causses
  (bluh day-coss)

Bleu du Haut Jura
  (bluh dew-oh-zhurah)

Bonbel
  (bon-bell)

Boursault
  (boor-so)

Boursin
  (boor-sen)

Brie
  (bree)

Brillat-Savarin
  (bree-ah sah-vah-ren)

Bûche Lorraine
  (bewsh lo-ren)

Bûcheron
  (bew-shuh-ron)

Camembert
(ka-ma*n*-**bare**)

Campagnole
(ca*n*-pah-**nyol**)

Cantal
(ca*n*-**tal**)

Caprice des Dieux
(cah-**preess** day **dyuh**)

Capricette
(cah-pree-**set**)

Carré de l'Est
(cah-ray duh **lest**)

Chabichou
(shah-bee-**shoo**)

Chaource
(shah-**oors**)

Chaumes
(shome)

Chevrotin
(sheh-vroh-te*n*)

Comté
(co*n*-tay)

Coulommiers
(coo-lum-**me-ay**)

Crottin de Chavignol
(cro-te*n* duh shah-vee-**nyohl**)

Délice de France
(day-lease duh **fra*n*se**)

Doux de Montagne
(do duh mo*n* **tah**-nyuh)

Emmental Français
(eh-me*n*-tall fra*n*-**seh**)

Epoisses
(ay-**pwahs**)

Ewe Rouergue
(oo roo-err-geh)

Fourme d'Ambert
(foorm d*an*-**bare**)

Gaperon
(gah-peh-ro*n*)

Géant du Poitou
(zhay-*an* dew pwah-**to**)

Gervais
(zher-**veh**)

Gourmandise
(goor-ma*n*-**deez**)

Gratte Paille
(graht **pah**-yuh)

La Bouille
(lah **boo**-yuh)

La Chevrette
(lah sheh-**vret**)

La Grappe
(lah grap)

Le Roulé
(luh roo-**lay**)

La Vache Qui Rit
(lah vash key **re**)

Lezay
(luh-**zay**)

Livarot
(lee-vah-**roe**)

Maroilles
(mah-**roy**)

Mimolette
(me-mo-**let**)

Monsieur Fromage
(muh-seeuh fro-**mazh**)

Montrachet
(mon-rah-**shay**) or (mon-trah-**shay**)

Morbier
(more-bee**ay**)

Neufchâtel
(nuf-shah-**tell**)

Petit Suisse
(ptee **sweess**)

Pipo Crem'
(pee-po **crem**)

Pont l'Evêque
(pon lay-**vek**)

Port Fleur
(pore fler)

Port Salut
(pore sal**yew**)

Pyramide
(pee-rah-**meed**)

Raclette
(rah-**clet**)

Rambol
(ran-**bole**)

Reblochon
(ruh-blo-**shon**)

Reybino
(ray-bee-**no**)

Roquefort
(rokuh-**for**)

Royal Provence
(rwa-yall pro-**vanss**)

Saint Julien
(sen zhew-**lyen**)

St. André
(sen tan-**dray**)

St. Marcellin
(se*n* mar-suh-**le***n*)

St. Paulin
(se*n* po-**le***n*)

Sainte Maure
(se*nt* **more**)

Saint Yves
(se*n* **teeve**)

Six de Savoie
(sees duh sah-**vwah**)

Soumaintrain
(soo-me*n*-tre*n*)

Suprême
(sue-**prem**)

Tomme des Pyrénées
(tum day pee-ray-**nay**)

Tomme de Savoie
(tum duh sah-**vwah**)

Tonnelait
(tonn-uh-leh)

Tourrée de l' Aubier
(tour-ay duh low-bee-**ay**)

Tourton
(tour-to*n*)

Valembert
(vah-la*n*-**bare**)

Vieux Pané
(vyuh pah-**nay**)

Les Vins/Wines & Terms

(lay-ve*n*)

Anjou
 (a*n*-**zhoo**)

Appellation Contrôlée
 (ah-pel-lah-**syo***n* co*n*-tro-**lay**)

Appellation d'Origine
 (ah-pel-lah-**syo***n* **doe**-re-**zheen**)

Apulia
 (ah-**pool**-ya)

Arbois
 (are-**bwah**)

Aude
 (ode)

Aurora
 (aw-**raw**-ra)

Ausone, Château
 (shah-toe ohs-**own**)

Auxey-Duresse
 (oak-say due-**ress**)

Bâtard-Montrachet
 (bah-**tar**-mo*n*-trah-**shay**)

Beaujolais
 (bo-zho-**leh**)

Beaumes-de Venise
 (bome duh ven-**neeze**)

Beaune
 (bone)

Bergerac
 (**bear**-zheh-**rack**)

Bienvenue-Bâtard-Montrachet
(be-*an*-vah-**new** bah-**tar** mo*n*-trah-**shay**)

Blagny
(blah-**nyee**)

Blanc de Noirs
(bla*n* duh **nwar**)

Blanc Fumé
(bla*n* few-**may**)

Blaye
(blay)

Bollinger
(ball-*en*-**zhay**)

Bonnes-Mares
(bun **mar**)

Bonnezeaux
(bun-**zoh**)

Bouchet
(boo-**sheh**)

Bourgeois
(boor-**zhwah**)

Bourgogne
(boor-**guh**-nyuh)

Bourgueil
(boor-**guh**-yuh)

Bouzy
(boo-**zee**)

Bressandes
(bres-**sa*n*d**)

Brouilly
(broo-**yee**)

Cabernet Franc
(cab-air-nay fre*n*)

Cahors
(cah-**or**)

Cailleret
(kigh-yuh-**ray**)

Cantenac
(ca*n*t-uh-**nack**)

Cassis
(cas-**sees**)

Cérons
(say-**ro***n*)

Chablis
(shab-**lee**)

Chalonnais
(shall-lon-**neh**)

Chambertin
(**sha***n*-bear-te*n*)

Chambolle-Musigny
(sha*n*-bol mew-zee-**knee**)

Champigny
(sha*n*-pee-**nyee**)

Chapelle-Chambertin
(sha-**pell** sha*n*-bare-te*n*)

Charmes-Chambertin
(sharm **sha***n*-bare-te*n*)

Chasselas
(shass-**la**)

Chassagne-Montrachet
(sha-**sanyuh** mo*n*-trah-**shay**)

Château-Chalon
(shah-toe **shah**-lo*n*)

Châteauneuf-du-Pape
(shah-toe-**nuff** dew **pap**)

Chelois
(shell-**wah**)

Chénas
(shay-**nahs**)

Cheval-Blanc, Château
(shvahl-**blan**)

Chevalier-Montrachet
(shev-al-**yay** mon-trah-**shay**)

Chorey-Les-Beaune
(shor-**ray**-lay-**bone**)

Chusclan
(shuse-clan)

Clos de Bèze
(clo duh **bezz**)

> **du Chapitre**
> (dew sha-**pee**-truh)

> **des Lambrays**
> (day lan-**bray**)

> **des Mouches**
> (day **moosh**)

> **de la Roche**
> (duh lah **rosh**)

> **du Roi**
> (dew **rwah**)

> **Saint-Denis**
> (sen duh-**nee**)

> **de Tart**
> (duh **tar**)

> **de Vougeot**
> (duh voo-zho)

Colombard
(co-lon-bar)

Combettes
(con-**bet**)

Condrieu
(con-dree-**yuh**)

Comptes de Champagne
(cont duh shan-**pan**-yuh)

Corbières
(cor-be-**yair**)

Corton-Charlemagne
(cor-to*n*-sharl-**man**-yuh)

Côte de Beaune-Villages
(coat duh **bone** vee-**lazh**)

> **de Brouilly**
> (duh broo-**yee**)

> **de Nuits**
> (duh **nwee**)

> **de Nuits-Villages**
> (duh **nwee** vee-**lazh**)

> **d'Or**
> (**door**)

> **Rotie**
> (ro-**tee**)

Coteaux Champenois
(co-toe sha*n*-pen-**wah**)

Coteaux du Layon
(co-**toe** dew lay-**yo*n***)

Coteaux du Tricastin
(co-**toe** dew tree-cas-te*n*)

Côtes de Bourg
(coat duh **boor**)

Côtes-du-Rhône
(coat dew **rone**)

Côtes du Ventoux
(coat dew va*n*-**too**)

Crépy
(cray-**pee**)

Criots-Bâtard-Montrachet
(cree-o bah-**tar** mo*n*-trah-**shay**)

Cristal
(cree-**stal**)

Crozes-Hermitage
(crows air-me-**tazh**)

Diamant Bleu
(dee-ama*n* **bluh**)

Dom Perignon
(do*n* pay-reen**yo***n*)

Dubonnet
(dew-bon-**nay**)

Échézeaux
(ay-shay-**zo**)

Épenots
(ay-pen-**no**)

Fitou
(fee-**too**)

Fumé Blanc
(few-may **bla***n*)

Gaillac
(gah-**yak**)

Gevrey-Chambertin
(jev-ray sha*n*-bear-**te***n*)

Gigondas
(**zhee**-gone-das)

Grands-Échezeaux
(gra*n*-zay-shay-**zo**)

Graves
(grahv)

Grèves
(grev)

Griotte-Chambertin
(gree-**ought**-sha*n*-bare-**te***n*)

Haut-Brion
(oh bree-**o***n*)

Haut-Médoc
(oh may-**dock**)

Hermitage
  (air-me-**tazh**)

Irroy
  (ear-**wah**)

Jacquesson
  (zhock-uh-**so**n)

Krug
  (crewg)

Ladoix-Serrigny
  (la-dwah serr-een-**yee**)

Lafite-Rothschild, Château
  (la-feet rot-**shield**)

Lanson
  (la**n**-so**n**)

Mâcon
  (mah-co**n**)

Mâcon-Fuissé
  (mah-**co**n fwee-**say**)

Malconsorts
  (mal-co**n**-**sore**)

Margaux, Château
  (shah-toe mar-**go**)

Marne et Champagne
  (marn ay sha**n**-**pan**-nyuh)

Massée
  (mass**ay**)

Mazis-Chambertin
  (ma-zee sha**n** bear-**te**n)

Mazoyères-Chambertin
  (ma-zwah-**yair**)

Médoc
  (may-**dock**)

Mercier
  (merse-**yay**)

Mercurey
(mare-cue-**ray**)

Merlot
(mair-**lo**)

Meursault
(mare-**so**)

Moët et Chandon
(mwet ay sha*n*-**do***n*)

Monbazillac
(mo*n*-ba-zee-**yack**)

Montagny
(**mo***n*-tan-**yee**)

Monthélie
(**mo***n*-tay-lee)

Montrachet
(mo*n*-rah-**shay**) or (mo*n*-trah-**shay**)

Morgeot
(more-**zho**)

Morgon
(more-go*n*)

Moulin-à-Vent
(**moo**-le*n* ah **va***n*)

Mourvèdre
(moor-**ved**-ruh)

Mouton-Rothschild, Château
(moo-**to***n* rot-**shield**)

Mumm
(moom)

Muscadelle
(muse-cah-**dell**)

Muscadet
(muse-cah-**day**)

Musigny
(mew-zeen-**ye**)

Nuits-Saint Georges
(nwee se*n* **zhorzh**)

Passe-Tout-Grains
(pahss too **gre***n*)

Pauillac
(po-**yack**)

Pécharmant
(pay-shar-**ma***n*)

Perrier-Jouet
(pair-**yay** zhoo-**ay**)

Petit Verdot
(ptee vair-**doe**)

Pétrus, Château
(shah-toe pay-**truce**)

Pineau des Charentes
(pee-no day shar-**ra***n*t)

Pinot
(pee-**no**)

Pinot Gris
(pee-**no gree**)

Pinot Noir
(pee-**no nwahr**)

Piper-Heidsick
(peapare-aidz**ick**)

Pomerol
(pom-uh-**roll**)

Pommard
(pom-**mar**)

Pommery
(pom-meh-**re**)

Pouilly-Fuissé
(poo-**ye** fwee-**say**)

Pouilly-Fumé
(poo-**ye** few-**may**)

Pouilly-sur-Loire
  (poo-**ye**-sewr-**lwahr**)

Pouilly-Vinzelles
  (poo-**ye** ve*n*-**zell**)

Pucelles
  (pew-s**ell**)

Puisseguin-Saint-Émilion
  (**pweess**-ge*n* sent ay-meel-**lyo***n*)

Puligny-Montrachet
  (pew-lean-ye mo*n*-trah-**shay**)

Quarts de Chaume
  (car duh **shome**)

Richebourg
  (reesh-**boor**)

Roederer, Louis
  (loo-**ee** roaderer)

Pol Roger
  (pole ruh-**zhay**)

Romanée-Conti
  (ro-ma-nay co*n*-**tee**)

Romanée-Saint-Vivant
  (ro-man-nay-se*n* vee-**va***n*)

Roussillon
  (rew-see-**yo***n*)

Ruchottes
  (rew-**shot**)

Rugiens
  (rew-**zhyen**)

Ruinart Pére et Fils
  (rwee-nar pair ay feess)

Rully
  (rew-**ye**)

Saint-Aubin
  (se*n*t oh-**be***n*)

Saint-Émilion
  (se*n* ay-meel-**lyo***n*)

Saint-Georges-Saint-Émilion
  (se*n* **zhorzh**)

Saint-Joseph
  (se*n* zho-**zeff**)

Saint-Péray
  (se*n* pay-**ray**)

Saint-Romain
  (se*n* ro-**me***n*)

Saint-Véran
  (se*n* vay-**ra***n*)

Sainte-Croix-du-Mont
  (se*n* crwa dew **mo***n*)

Sancerre
  (se*n*-**sair**)

Sauternes
  (so-**tairn**)

Savigny-Les-Beaune
  (**sav**-eenyee lay-**bone**)

Seyssel
  (say-**sell**)

Tâche, La
  (lah-tosh)

Taittinger
  (tay-te*n*-zhay)

Tavel
  (tah-**vel**)

Veuve Cliquot
  (vuv cleeko)

Vin de Pays
  (ve*n*-duh-**payee**)

Viré
  (vee-**ray**)

Volnay
(vull-**nay**)

Vosne-Romanée
(vone ro-mah-**nay**)

Vougeot
(voo-**zho**)

GERMAN

Food and Wine

Die Art der Zubereitung von Speisen in der Küche/Culinary Terms

(dee art dare soober-**eye**-tongue fawn shpy-zen in dare kook-eh)

Am Spies/on a skewer
(am shpees)

Bitter/bitter
(bitter)

Butter/butter
(boot-ter)

Einbrenne/butter-flour paste
(**ine**-bren-eh)

Estrogon/tarragon
(estra-gone)

Farcieren/stuffed
(far-**seer**en)

Feine Kräuter/herb mixture
(fie-neh croyter)

Garnieren/garnished
(gar-**neer**en)

Gebräunte butter/browned in butter
(geh-broynt-eh boot-ter)

Gefüllt/filled
(geh-foolt)

Gehackt/chopped
(geh-hawkt)

Geräucherte/fish or vegetable stock
(geh-royk-erteh)

Gespickt/meat inserted with fat strips
(geh-shpeekt)

Gewürzt/spiced
(geh-voorst)

Heiss/hot
(highss)

Imbiss/snack
(im beess)

Kalt/cold
(calt)

Knödel/fish or meat dumplings
(knoodle ("oo" as in cook))

Knochenlos/boneless fish
(knock (pronounce the first "k")-en-los)

Mariniert/marinated
(marin-yeert)

Milch/with milk
(meelk)

Naturell/plain
(na-tour-el)

Panieren/coated with crumbs
(pan-eeren)

Roh/raw
(roe)

Sauer/sour
(sower)

Schaumig/foamy
(show-mig ("o" as in how))

Schwarzer kaffee/black coffee
(shvartser caffay)

Speck/fat
(shpeck)

Sülze/in aspic
(soolts-eh)

Torte/custard tart
(tort-eh)

Wurst/sausage
(voorst)

Die art der Zubereitung der Speisen Cooking Methods

(dee art dare soober-**eye**-tongue dare shpy-zen)

Angekocht/blanched
  (onguh-coct)

Auf der Platte gebräunt/browned on top
  (off dare pla-teh **geh**-broynt)

Gebacken im ofen/baked in the oven
  (geh-backen im ohfen)

Gebraten/fried
  (geh-brotten)

Gedämpft/stewed
  (geh-**demft)**

Gedünstet/braised
  (geh-dun-stet)

Gerösted/roasted
  (geh-**roo**-sted ("oo" as in cook))

Gesiedet/boiled
  (geh-zee-det)

Im feuer gebraten/grilled
  (im foyer geh-brotten)

In der Pfanne abgebraten/browned in a frying pan
  (fannuh ab-**geh**-brotten)

In Dunst gekocht/poached
  (doonst geh-coct)

In schmalz gebacken/French fries
  (shmalts geh-bocken)

Langsam gekocht/slow cooked
  (long-sam **geh**-coct)

Langsam gesotten/slowly simmered
  (long-sam geh-zotten)

Schnell gebraten/quick fried
  (shnel geh-brotten)

Serviert in der Brühe/served in its broth
  (serv-yert in dare brew-eh)

Saucen/Sauces

(zowsen)

Allemande
  (alla-mond)

Björn Björnson
  (b-yorn b-yornsen)

Bordelaiser
  (bore-deh-lazer)

Burgunder
  (boor-goonder)

Feine Kräuter
  (fie-neh croyter)

Fischgrund
  (fish-groond)

Holländische
  (hollon-deesh-eh)

Hummer
  (hoomer)

Indischer Curry
  (**in**-deesh-er)

Italienische
  (italia-neesh-eh)

Kapern
  (capern)

Maître de Butter
  (maytruh dee boot-ter)

Pikante Meerrittich
  (pee-contay mare-**ret**ick)

Rouenneser
  (ruin-eezer)

Senf
  (zenf)

Smetana
  (smetana)

Tataren
  (ta-**tar**-ren)

Tiroler
  (tee-**roller**)

Venezianer
  (ven-ets-yanner)

Von Schwarzen Johannisbeeren
  (fawn shvartsen yohannis-bairen)

Weisse
  (vice-eh)

Zwiebel
  (swee-bel)

Die Stile der Zubereitung von Gerichten in der Küche/Styles of Food Preparation

(dee shteel-eh dare soober-eye-tongue fawn geh-rikten in dare kook-eh)

Arnold Bucklin
(boo-klin)

Bayrischer
(by-**rish**-er)

Berliner Art
(bare-**leaner**)

Edel Pilze
(aidle **peel**-seh)

Eisenhut, à la
(**eye**-zun-hoot)

Ervin von Steinbach
(airvin fawn shtine-bock)

Frieda Hempel
(freeda hem-**pell**)

Frikadellen
(freak-a-dellen)

Gedämpftes Rindfleisch
(geh-dampftes **reend**-flysh)

Gesottene Rinderbrust
(geh-zotten-eh reender-broost)

Helene
(hell-**ay**-nay)

Holstein, à la
(hole-shtyne)

Kaiser Schmarren
(shmar-ren)

Kasseler Rippchen
(cassler reep-**ken**)

Königin Elisabeth
(**coin**-again ay-leeza-**bet**)

Königsberger Klopse
(**coin**-igs-burger clup-seh)

Kotelette à la Hubertus
(hoo-bairtus)

Krebs Schwanze
(**shven**-seh)

Linne
(*lee*-nay)

Munchner
(**moonk**-ner)

Natur
(na-**tour**)

Prince Marschal Blucher
(mar-**shall bloo**sher)

Rheinischer
(rine-**ish**-er)

Rinderschmorbraten
(reender-**shmore**-brotten)

Rindsrouladen
(reends-roo-**lahden**)

Sauerbraten
(**zower**-brotten)

Schinkenröllchen mit Spargel
(**shinken**-rull-ken mit shpargel)

Schlemmerrolle
(**shlem**-er-roll-eh)

Schweinshaxe
(shvine-**hacks**-ee)

Schweinsfilets mit Saurer Sahne
(shwines-fee-lay mit zowrer zah-**nay**)

Tiroler
(tee-**roller**)

Walter Spiel
(vaulter-sh**peel**)

Wiener Schnitzel
(**veen**-ur)

Zwiebelfleisch
(swee-bel-**flysh**)

Vorspeisen/Hors-d'oeuvres
(for-shpyzen)

Aal-Roulade
(ahl-roo-**lah**-deh)

Austern Bernadotte
(**ow-**stern burn-a-dot)

Austern Pastetchen
(**ow**-stern pa-**street**-ken)

Der Hummer, geröstet, Amerikanische Art
(dur hoomer geh-roastet amera-canisha art)

Die Auster
(dee ouster)

Die Krevette
(dee crevet-eh)

Eier Bombay
(ire bombay)

Eingelegter herring mit meerrettich
(ine-gelegter herring mit mare-**ret**ick)

Gebacken mit feinen Kräutern
(geh-backen mit fie-nen croy-tern)

Herring salat
(sa-lot)

Herring salat finnische art
(feenish-eh)

Hummer à la Siegheim
(hoomer ah lah seeg-hime)

Kalte Forelle de krebs au naturell
(callta for-elly dee crebs oh na-tour-ell)

Krebs Schwanze Walter Spiel
(crebs schvent-seh vaulter shpeel)

Melone mit Krebs Schwänzchen
(shvents-shen)

Räucher lachs
(roysher lox)

Tartelette mit Froschkeulen
(frosh-coilen)

Tartelette mit Kalbs Hirn
(tarta-letta mit calbs heern)

Vorspeise Greta Garbo
(for-shpypzeh grayta garbo)

Uberkrustet, Villeroi
(oober-crew-stet viller-rwah)

Geback/Breads
(geh-bock)

Brötchen/roll
  (broatken)

Kipfel/croissant
  (keepfel)

Roggenbrot/rye bread
  (roggen-broat)

Schwarzbrot/black bread
  (shvarts-broat)

Semmel/roll
  (zemmel)

Weissbrot/white bread
  (vice-broat)

Suppen/Soups
(zoopen)

Erbsen Suppe
  (airbzen zoopeh)

Erdäpfel
  (air-dep-fel)

Frosch
  (fro-sh)

Fisch
  (fish)

Geflügel Kraftbruhe
  (geh-flugle craft-**brew**-yeh)

Gemüse
  (geh-moo-zeh)

Gesundheit
  (geh-**zoont**-hite)

Grüne Erbsen
  (groon-eh-airbzen)

Kalte Kraftbrühe à la Madrilene
  (caltay craft-**brew**-yeh ah lah mad-re-len)

Kalte Kraftbrühe Portugiesische Art
  (caltay craft-**brew**-yeh porta**geez**isha)

Kalte Kraftbrühe Russische Art
  (caltay craft-**brew**-yeh roo-**see**-shuh)

Kalte Kraftbrühe Schaljapin
  (caltay craft-**brew**-yeh shall-yawpeen)

Kraftbrühe à la Hausfrauen Art
  (craft-**brew**-yeh ah lah **house**-frown)

Krebs
  (crebs)

Legierte Rebhühner
  (Lay-**gair**-teh rayb-hooner ("oo" as in cook))

Legierte Schildkröten
  (lay-**gair**-teh shild-crooten ("oo" as in cook))

Legierte Schnepfen
  (lay-**gair**-teh shnepfen)

Legierte Tauben
  (Lay-**gair**-teh (Tauben rhymes with cow-ben))

Linsen
  (linzen)

Zwiebel/onion
  (zweeble)

Fleisch und Wildbret/
Meat and Game

(flysh oond vildbret)

Bär/bear
 (bare)

Hase/wild hare
 (hah-zeh)

Hirschbraten/roast venison
 (heersh-brotten)

Jünger hase/young hare
 (yoonger-**hah**-zeh)

Jüngschwein/suckling pig
 (yoong-shvine)

Kalbfleisch/veal
 (calb-flysh)

Kaninchen/rabbit
 (can-**in**-ken)

Lamm/lamb
 (lom)

Reh/deer
 (ray)

Rehbock/roe-buck
 (raybock)

Rehbraten/roast venison
 (ray-brotten)

Rindfleisch/beef
 (rind (rhymes with sinned)-flysh)

Schinken/ham
 (shinken)

Schweinefleisch/pork
 (**shvine**-eh-flysh)

Schweine schlegel/fresh pork leg
  (shvine-eh shlaygel)

Wildschwein/wild boar
  (vild-shvine)

Ziege/goat
  (zee-geh)

Teilung des Fleisches/
Meat Cuts

(tie-loong des flyshes)

Bries/sweetbreads
  (breese)

Flugel/wing
  (floogel)

Hirn/brains
  (heern)

Jäger fleisch/brisket
  (yayger flysh)

Kalbsbrust/calf breast
  (colbs-broost)

Knöchel/shank
  (knookle ("oo" as in look))

Kotelett/chops
  (coat-eh-let)

Kuttel fleisch/tripe
  (kootle flysh)

Leber/liver
  (labor)

Lungen-oder Lenden Braten/tenderloin
  (loongen oder lenden brotten)

Nieren/kidney
  (nearen)

Ochsenschwanz/tail
  (oxen-shvonce)

Rind Schnitzen/smaller than medallions
  (rind[rhymes with sinned]shnitsen)

Rindfleisch/steak
  (rind[rhymes with sinned]-flysh)

Rippen/ribs
  (rippen)

Rostbraten/joint
  (roast-bratten)

Rücken/saddle
  (rook-en)

Schnitzel/medallions
  (shnits-el)

Schweinsleber/pork liver
  (shvines-labor)

Speck/fat
  (shpeck)

Spitzenfleisch/top of round
  (shpeetsin-flysh)

Würstchen/little sausages
  (veerst-ken)

Zunge/tongue
  (soong-eh)

Geflügel/Fowl

(geh-flugel)

Backhuhn/little fryer
(bock-hoon)

Brathuhn/roasting chicken
(brot-hoon)

Drossel/thrush
(drossel)

Ente/duck
(en-tay)

Fasan/pheasant
(fa-zan)

Gans/goose
(ganss)

Hahn/rooster
(hahn)

Jünge ente/duckling
(yoong-geh en-tay)

Jünges huhn/young chicken, a fryer
(yoonges-hoon)

Jünger truthahn/young turkey
(yoonger troot-hahn)

Kapaun/capon
(cap-oun)

Perlhuhn/guinea hen
(pearl-hoon)

Rebhuhn/partridge
(rayb-hoon)

Schnepfe/woodcock
(**shnep**-feh)

Taube/pidgeon
  (rhymes with **cow** bay)

Truthahn/turkey
  (troot-hahn)

Wachtel/quail
  (vahk-tel)

Waldhuhn/grouse
  (vauld-hoon)

Fische, muscheln und krebse/
Fish, Mollusks and Shellfish

(feesh-eh, moosh-eln und crebs-eh)

Aal/eel
  (all)

Auster/oyster
  (ouster)

Barsch/perch
  (barsh)

Crevette/shrimp
  (crevet-eh)

Flunder/flounder
  (floonder)

Forelle/trout
  (for-elly)

Frosch/frog
  (fro-sh)

Hecht/pike
  (hekt)

Hummer/lobster
  (hoomer)

Kabeljau/cod
  (cabble-yow)

Karpfen/carp
  (carpfen)

Krabbe/crawfish
  (crab-eh)

Krebse/crab
  (crebs-eh)

Lachsforelle/salmon trout
  (lox-for-ell-eh)

Languste/spiny lobster
  (lan-goost-eh)

Makrele/mackerel
  (ma-crell-eh)

Muscheln/clam
  (moosh-eln)

Muscheln/mussel
  (moosh-eln)

Kleine schussel/scallops
  (cline-eh shoosel)

Salm/salmon
  (solm)

Sardelle/anchovy
  (sardel-ay)

Sardinen/sardine
  (zur-deenen)

Schildkröte/turtle
  (shild-croot-eh ("oo" as in cook))

Schleie/schleie
  (shly-eh)

See-aal/sea eel, conger eel
  (see-all)

See-barsch/sea bass
  (see-barsh)

See-igel/sea urchin
  (sea-eagle)

Seezunge/sole
  (see-soong-eh)

Stearlet/stearlet
  (stare-let)

Steinbutt/turbot
  (shtyn-boot)

Thunfisch/tuna
 (toon-fish)

Tintenfisch/squid
 (tinten-fish)

Zander/zander
 (sander)

Die Art der Zubereitung der Eier Gerichte/Eggs-Cooking Methods

(dee art dare soober-eye-tongue dare ire geh-reesh-teh)

Auflauf/omelette
  (owf-loff)

Eier auf Amerikanische Art/American-style fried eggs
  (amera-canisha)

Eier in cocotte/eggs in ramekins
  (ire in co-cot)

Eier speise/scrambled eggs
  (ire shpys-eh)

Gebackene eier/grilled eggs
  (geh-bocken-eh ire)

Hart gekocht eier/hard boiled eggs
  (hart geh-coct ire)

Poschiert/poached eggs
  (poe shairt)

Ruhreier/scrambled eggs
  (roor-ire)

Spiegel eier/friend eggs
  (shpy-gel ("g" as in gun))

Weiche eier/soft boiled eggs
  (vike-eh)

Gëmuse und Schwämme/
Vegetables and Fungi

(geh-moo-zeh und shwemm-eh)

Artischocke/artichoke
  (artie-**shaw**-kay)

Blumenkohl/cauliflower
  (bloomen-coal)

Bohnen/beans
  (bonen)

Bohnen, gelbe/yellow beans
  (gelb-eh bonen)

Bohnen, grüne/green beans
  (grew-nuh bonen)

Brunnenkresse/watercress
  (broonen-**cress**-eh)

Champignon/mushrooms
  (shamp-**een**-yon)

Endivie/endive
  (an-deevee)

Gerste/barley
  (gair-steh)

Gruner salat/lettuce
  (groon-err sa-lot)

Gurke/cucumber
  (goor-keh)

Karotte/carrots
  (car-ought-eh)

Kartoffeln/potatoes
  (car-toffeln)

Knoblauch/garlic
  (kno-blouk)

Kohl/cabbage
  (coal)

Kohlrabi/kohlrabi
  (cole-**robby**)

Lauch/leeks
  (louk)

Linse/lentil
  (lean-zeh)

Meerrettich/horseradish
  (mare-**ret**ick)

Petersilie/parsley
  (payter-zealia)

Pfeffergurke/gherkin
  (feffer-goor-keh)

Pfeffer/peppers
  (feffer)

Pfeffer, roter/red peppers
  (roter feffer)

Rettig/radish
  (rettig)

Rosenkohl/brussel sprouts
  (rozen-coal)

Rübe/turnips
  (rube-eh)

Runkelrübe/beets
  (roonkle-rube-eh)

Sauerampfer/sorrel
  (zower-ampfur)

Schalotte/shallot
  (shall-ought-eh)

Schoten/peas
  (show-tn)

Schoten, grüne/green peas
  (groon-eh show-tn)

Sellerie/celery
  (celery)

Schnittlauch/chive
  (shnit-louk)

Spargel/asparagus
  (shpargel)

Spinat/spinach
  (shpee-nat)

Tomate/tomato
  (toe-maht-eh)

Trüffel/truffles
  (troof-fel)

Zwiebel/onions
  (swee-bel)

Süss-Speisen/Desserts

(zoos shpy-zen)

Apfel Beignets/apple pastry
  (**ap**-fel bane-yea)

Apfel Strudel/apple strudel
  (**ap**-fel shtroodel)

Auflauf/dessert soufflé
  (owf-loff)

Blatterteig/puff pastry
  (blatter-tig (as in tiger))

Brät Apfel/baked apple
  (brat **ap**-fel)

Creme Schnitten/puff pastry
  (cream shnitten)

Gefrorenes/ices and ice creams
  (geh-fror-ren-ess)

Gestürzte Weincreme/zabaglione
  (gez-terse-teh vine-crem-eh)

Kleine Eier Kuchen/petite fours
  (cline-eh ire **coo**-ken)

Krapfen/donuts
  (crapfen)

Obstkuchen/fruit cake
  (obst-**coo**-ken)

Salzburger Nockerl/"floating islands"
  meringue
  (zalls-burger knockearl)

Zwetschgen Kuchen/prune cake
  (swaych-gen)

Früchte/Fruits

(frook-teh)

Ananas/pineapple
(ana-noss)

Apfel/apple
(**ap**-fell)

Apfelsinnen/oranges
(ap-fell-zeenen)

Aprikosen/apricot
(apry-**co**-zen)

Banane/banana
(banan-eh)

Beeren/berry
(bairen)

Birnen/pear
(bernen)

Brombeeren/blackberry
(brom-bairen)

Erdbeeren/strawberry
(aird-bairen)

Feigen/fig
(fie-gen ("g" as in gun))

Himbeeren/rasberry
(heem-bairen)

Johannisbeeren/red currants
(yo-**honnis**-bairen)

Kirschen/cherry
(**keer**-shen)

Kürbis/pumpkin
(coorbis)

Marillen/apricot
  (ma-reelen)

Melonen/melon
  (mel-**oh**-nen)

Olive/olive
  (oh-**leave**-eh)

Pampelmusen/grapefruit
  (pampel-moozen)

Pflaumen/prunes
  (flowmen (rhymes with ploughmen))

Pfirsiche/peaches
  (fears-**eeka**)

Preiselbeeren/cranberries
  (pryzle-bairen)

Quitten/quince
  (quitten)

Rosinen/raisin
  (roe-**zee**-nen)

Trauben/grapes
  ((trauben rhymes with browben))

Stachelbeeren/gooseberries
  (shtockle-bairen)

Zitrone/lemon
  (see-trone-eh)

Zwetchgen/plum
  (svetch-gen)

Käse/Cheeses

(cays-eh)

Allgaeuer Kaese
  (algower)

Bayernland Butterkaese
  (by-**earn**-land boot-ter-cays-eh)

Bergader
  (burr-gadder)

Blauschimmelkaese
  (blough-shimmel-cays-eh)

Buesumer Markenkaese
  (be-zoomer marken cays-eh)

Deutscher Edamer Bayernland
  (doycher aydamer by-**earn**-land)

Deutscher Emmenthaler
  (doycher emen-taller)

Ditmarscher Landkaese
  (ditmarsher land-cays-eh)

Edelweiss Brie
  (aidle-vice)

Gut von Holstein
  (goot fawn hole-shtyne)

Handkaese
  (hond-cays-eh)

Harzer Kaese
  (harser)

Hindelanger Spitzbub
  (hind-eh (as in hinder)-longer spits-boob)

Hochlandkaese
  (hockland cays-eh)

Holtsee
(holt-say)

Karwendel Kaese
(car-vendel)

Kochkaese
(coke-cays-eh)

Mainzer Kaese
(mine-zer)

Molfseer
(molf-sare)

Räucherkaese einfach
(royker-cays-eh ine-fock)

Schmelzkaese
(shmelts-cays-eh)

Steppenkaese
(shteppen-cays-eh)

Tilsiter
(tell-sitter)

*The "kaese" suffix on many of these names is the old fashioned spelling of "käse."

Die Weine/Wines

(dee vine-eh)

Ahr
(are)

Anbaugebiet
(**ohn**-bough-geh-beet)

Avelsbach
(**ah**-vuhls-bock)

Beerenauslese
(bairen-**ouse**-lay-zeh)

Bereich
(beh-**rike**)

Bocksbeutel
(**bocks**-boy-tul)

Brauneberg
(**brown**-eh-bairg)

Deidesheim
(**die**-dess-hime)

Dhron
(drone)

Durkeim
(**deerk**-hime)

Eiswein
(**ice**-vine)

Gewurztraminer
(geh-**vertz**-tram-**me**-ner)

Huxelrebe
(**hoo**-sel-ray-beh)

Johannisberg
(yo-**hahn**-nis-bairg)

Mosel
(**mose**-l)

Moselblumchen
(**mose**-l-**blum**-shen)

Muller-Thurgau
(**mah**-ler **ter**-gow)

Neumagen
(**noy**-mog-en)

Niederhausen
(**nee**-der-how-zen)

Nierstein
(**near**-shtine)

Oestrich
(**uhs**-trich)

Piesport
(**peas**-port)

Qualitatswein
(kval-ee-tots-vine)

Rauenthal
(rhymes with **brow**-en-tall)

Rheingau
(**rine**-gow)

Rheinpfalz
(**rine**-faults)

Rudesheim
(**roo**-dess-hime)

Ruwer
(**roo**-ver)

Scharzhofberg
(**shartz**-hawf-bairg)

Schaumwein
(**shome**-vine)

Scheurebe
(**shoy**-ray-beh)

Schillerwein
  (**shel**-ler-vine)

Schloss Bockelheim
  (shlawss **bok**-el-hime)

Spatlese
  (**shpat**-lay-zeh)

Steinberg
  (**shtine**-bairg)

Traminer
  (tram-**me**-ner)

Vollrads, Schloss
  (**fall**-rods)

Wehlen
  (**vay**-len)

ITALIAN

Food and Wine

Nomenclatura Culinaria/
Culinary Terms

(no-men-**kla**-toora
cool-**een**-aria)

Aceto/vinegar
 (ah-ch**ay**toe)

Affumicato/smoked
 (afoomy-**cot**-oh)

Aglio/garlic
 (**all**-yo)

Agro/sour
 (aw-grow)

Al Dente/chewy texture
 (**den**-tay)

Amaro/bitter
 (ah-**mar**-oh)

Ben cotto/well done
 (ben-**cot**-toe)

Bianco/white
 (be-**on**co)

Bolliti misti/boiled meat
 (bo-**lee**-tee misty)

Brodo/broth
 (**braw**-doe)

Burro/butter
 (**boor**-roe)

Caffè liscio/black coffee
 (ka-fay lee-show)

Caldo/hot
 (call-doe)

Capperi/capers
(cap-**pair**-ee)

Carrozza, in/in crust
(car-**rots**-ah)

Conchiglia/shell
(con-**keel**-ya)

Condimento/dressing, seasoning
(con-dee-**men**-to)

Crostino/toast
(**crow**-steeno)

Crudo/raw
(crew-**doe**)

Cuscinetti/baked cheese rolls
(coo-she-**net**-tee)

Doppio/double strength
(dawpio)

Farsumagru/forcemeat
(far-**sue-maw**-grew)

Freddo/cold
(fred-doe)

Fresco/fresh
(fresco)

Gelatina/jelly
(jay-**la**-tina)

Ginepro/juniper
(jee-**nay**-pro)

Latte/milk
(lah-**tay**)

Maceratese/smothered
(match-**aira**-tayzee)

Magro/lean
(**maw**-grow)

Mandorle/almonds
(mon-**door**-lay)

Marmellata/preserves
(mar-**may**-lotta)

Midollo/marrow
(me-**dole**-uh)

Misto/mixed
(meesto)

Nero/black
(nayro)

Noci/walnuts
(**no**-chee)

Nocciole/hazel nuts
(naw-**chaw**-lay)

Olio d' oliva/olive oil
(awlyo-doe-leeva)

Osso/bone
(aw-**so**)

Panna/cream
(**pan**-nah)

Panna montata/whipped cream
(mon-**tah**-tah)

Pepe/pepper
(pay**pay**)

Peperonata/fried peppers
(paypay-roe-**nah**-ta)

Piccante/spicy
(pick-**con**-tay)

Polpette/meat balls
(pol-**pay**-tay)

Rafano/horse radish
(**ra**-fan-oh)

Ragù/meat and tomato sauce
(**raw**-goo)

Risi e bisi/Venetian rice and peas
(reezy ay beezy)

Rosa/pink
  (roe-**zuh**)

Rosso/red
  (**ross**-so)

Sale/salt
  (**saw**-lay)

Salmi/way of preparing game
  (sal-**me**)

Salsicce/sausage
  (sal-**see**-chay)

Salvia/sage
  (**sal**-vee-ah)

Senapa/mustard
  (**sen**-ah-puh)

Sfogliata/thin pastry
  (**sfoal**-yaw-ta)

Spezzatino/stew
  (spetz-**a**-tino)

Sugo/gravy
  (sue-go)

Tritato/chopped
  (tree-**tah**-toe)

Umido/stew
  (**oomy**-doe)

Verde/green
  (**vare**-day)

Verdure/green vegetables
  (vare-**dure**-ay)

Zenzero/ginger
  (**zen**-zare-oh)

Metodi di Cottura/Cooking Methods

(met-**oh**-dee dee co-toora)

Affogate/poached
  (a-foe-**gah**-tay)

Affumicato/smoked
  (a-foomy-**cot**-oh)

Arrosto/baked
  (a-**rahst**-o)

Bianco, in/plain
  (in be-onco)

Bollito/boiled
  (bo-leeto)

Bollito lento/slow boiled
  (len-toe)

Diavolo, alla/broiled
  (dee-**a**-volo)

Fiamma, alla/flamed
  (fee-ama)

Forno, al/casserole baking
  (**for**-no)

Fritto/fried
  (**freet**-toe)

Fritto, al fuoco vivo/quick fried
  (foo-ohco veevo)

Fritto in tegame/pan fried
  (tay-**gam**-ay)

Griglia, alla/grilled
  (**greel**-ya)

Lesso/boiled meat
  (**leh**-so)

Patate fritte/french fries
  (pa-tah-tay free-**tay**)

Patate lesse/steamed potatoes
  (les-**say**)

Stufato/braised
  (stoo-fah-toe)

Salse/Sauces

(**sal**-say)

Agrodolce
(awgro-**dole**-chay)

Alemanna
(all-ay-**man**-a)

Amatriciana, all'
(ahma-tree-**chana**)

Andalusa, all'
(an-dal-**oo**-za)

Bastarda
(bass-**tar**-da)

Bearnese
(bear-**nay**-zay)

Besciamella
(bay-**sha**-mell-la)

Boscaiola, alla
(bose-kigh-**oh**-la)

Bruna
(br**oo**na)

Carbonara
(car-bo-nara)

Carrettiera, alla
(car-et-tee-**aira**)

Diavola, alla
(dee-**a**-vula)

Finanziera, alla
(fee-nan-zee-**ar**-ra)

Fiorentina, alla
(fee-**or**-en-**tee**-na)

Infernale
  (in-fir-**nal**-ay)

Maionese
  (my-own-**ay**-zay)

Monegasca, alla
  (moan-ay-**ga**ska)

Mousseline
  (moose-el-**ee**-nay)

Olandese
  (all-on-**day**-zay)

Palermitana, alla
  (pal-air-me-**ta**wna)

Perugina, alla
  (pay-roo-**zhee**na)

Pesto
  (**pay**-stow)

Peverata
  (pay-vair-**ah**-ta)

Piemontese, alla
  (pee-ay-mon-**tay**zay)

Provenzale, alla
  (pro-ven-**saul**-ay)

Spagnola, alla
  (span-**yolla**)

Siciliana, alla
  (see-chill-**ya**na)

Spoletina, alla
  (spole-ay-**ti**na)

Ungherese, all'
  (oong-gare-**ay**zay)

Maniere di Preparazione/Styles of Preparation

(man-**yera** dee preh-par-**atzy**-own-ay)

Abruzzese, all'
  (a-brutes-**say**zay)

Anconetana, all'
  (an-cone-ay-**tawn**-a)

Assisiana, all'
  (ah-seezy-**anna**)

Borghese, alla
  (bore-**gay**zay)

Brodetato
  (bro-day-**tah**-toe)

Cacciatora, alla
  (ca-cha-**tora**)

Cipriani, alla
  (chee-pre-**annie**)

Della nonna
  (day-la **no**-na)

Genovese, alla
  (jayno-vayzay)

Giardino, al
  (jardino)

Giordano
  (jor-**danno**)

Imperiali San Giusto
  (em-perry-**al**-lee san joosto)

Ligure, alla
  (**lee**-gooray)

Livornese
(lee-vor-**nay**zay)

Mantovana, alla
(mon-toe-**va**na)

Massimiliano, alla
(mass-see-mealy-**ano**)

Napoletana
(na-**poley**-tana)

Novecento Quattro
(**no**-vay-chento)

Pavese
(pa-**vay**-zay)

Perugina
(pay-**roo**-jeena)

Piatto, al
(**pee**-a-toe)

Pizzaiola, alla
(peets-eye-**oh**-la)

Richard
(**reach**-urd)

Romagnola, alla
(ro-**man**-yolla)

Romana, alla
(roe-**mana**)

Toscana
(**toe**-scana)

Trasimeno, di
(trazzy-**man**-no)

Triestina, alla
(tree-es-**tee**-na)

Veneziana, alla
(venets-ee-**ah**-na)

Vesuviana, alla
(vay-sue-vyana)

Vicentina, alla
(vee-chen-**tee**-na)

Antipasti/Appetizers

(antee-pastee)

Antipasto di crostini/cheese crusts
(**crow**-steeny)

Antipasto di primavera/spring salad
(prima-vaira)

Bagna cauda/anchovy dip
(banya cowduh)

Bocconcini fritti/finger food
(buh-**con**-cheeny **free**-tea)

Cestini di uova sode/eggs in tomato
"baskets"
(chesteeny dee wove-ah **saw**day)

Crostini di pomodoro/tomato cheese crusts
(crowsteeny)

Crostini con salsa di alici/cheese crust with
anchovy sauce
(crowsteeny con salsa dee aleechy)

Prosciutto e melone/melon and ham
(pro-**shoe**-toe ay mel-**own**-ay)

Peperoncini sott 'olio/peppers in oil
(pay-**pay**-ron-cheeny sote tollio)

Tartine di Mortadella/bread slices with
baloney
(tar-teenay dee morta-dayla)

Uova ripiene/stuffed eggs
(**wove**-ah ree-pyaynah)

Vitello tonnato/veal with tuna sauce
(veetello **toe**-natto)

Pasta

(pahsta)

Bucatini
(boo-ca-teenie)

Cannelloni
(can-**nay**-loan-ay)

Capelli d'Angelo
(ca-**pay**-lee **dan**-jullo)

Cappellacci
(ca-**pell**-otchy)

Fettuccine
(fay-to-**chee**-nay)

Frascarelli
(fras-car-**aily**)

Fusilli
(foo-**zeal**-lee)

Gnocchi
(naw-**key**)

Lasagne
(law-**zon**-yuh)

Linguini
(ling-**gwee**nie)

Maltagliati
(moll-**tal**-yawty)

Orecchiette
(aura-**key**-et-**tay**)

Pappardelle
(paw-par-**dell**-lay)

Penne
(**pay**-nuh)

Ravioli
  (rah-**vio**-lee)

Raviolini
  (rah-**vio**-lini)

Risotto
  (re-**zot**-toe)

Rosellini
  (roe-**zay**-lini)

Stracci
  (stratchy)

Strete
  (**stray**-tay)

Tagliatelle
  (tal-**ya**-tell-ay)

Taglierini
  (tal-**yea**-reenee)

Tortellini
  (tortuh-**lee**-knee)

Pane/Breads

(pah-**nay**)

Biscotti di Prato
   (bee-scotty dee **pra**-toe)

Focaccia
   (fo-cah-cha)

Grissino
   (gree-seeno)

Pandoro

Panettone di Milano
   (panna-toe-nay dee me-lano)

Pitte con Nepita
   (pee-**tay** con **neh**-pee-tah)

Pizza Calabrese
   (cala-brayzay)

Pizza Napoletana
   (na-**po**-laytana)

Pizza Pasquale alla Triestina
   (pa-**squall**-ay)

Schiacciata alla Fiorentina
   (ski-a-chotta alla fee-or-en-**tina**)

Minestra (or zuppa)/Soup

(mean-**ess**-trah, zoopah)

Note: not listed here are the many soups named after ingredients that appear under other headings, e.g. Vegetables, Pasta or Meats. Also omitted are soups whose names are listed under Styles of Preparation.

Cucolo, alla
 (**kook**-ulloh)

Minestrone
 (mean-**ess**-tronay)

Paparot
 (pa-**pa**-rot)

Stracciatella
 (stratch-a-tayla)

Valdostana, alla
 (voldostana)

Verbanese, alla
 (vare-**ban**-ayzay)

Verdure, di
 (vair-**dure**-uh)

Carni e Selvaggina/Meat and Game

(carny ay sell-vajeena)

Agnello/lamb
  (**an**-yellow)

Bue/ox
  (boo-**eh**)

Capra/goat
  (capra)

Capriolo/roe-buck
  (capriolo)

Carne di cervo/vension
  (carnay-dee-**chair**-voh)

Carne di maiale/pork
  (carnay-**dee**-my-alley)

Carne secca/air-dried salt beef
  (carnay **say**-cuh)

Cinghiale/boar
  (ching-**gee**-alley (gee as in geek))

Coniglio/rabbit
  (cone-eelyo)

Lepre/wild hare
  (**leh**-pray)

Manzo/beef
  (man-**zoe**)

Montone/mutton
  (mon-**tone**-ay)

Porcellino/suckling pig
  (porch-**ay**-leeno)

Vitello/veal
  (vee-**tello**)

Tagli di carne/Meat Cuts

(**tal**-yee dee carnay)

Ali/wing
(ah-**lee**)

Animelle/sweetbreads
(ony-**mell**-lay)

Bistecca/steak
(be-**stake**-a)

Braciolone/chops
(bra-**cho**-loan-ay)

Cervella/brains
(chur-vella)

Cima/top of the round
(cheema)

Coda/tail
(**co**-da)

Costole/ribs
(cost-**oh**-lay)

Costolette/medallions
(cost-oh-**let**-tay)

Cotolette/cutlets
(co-toe-**lay**-tay)

Fegatelli/slices of pork liver
(**fay**-ga-telly)

Fegato/liver
(**fay**-ga-toe)

Filetto/tenderloin
(fee-**let**-toe)

Giuntura/joint
(jun-**tour**-a)

Lingua/tongue
(leengwa)

Lombo/loin
(lum-**bo**)

Lombo di manzo/sirloin
(monzo)

Pancetta/bacon
(pan-chay-ta)

Petto/breast
(peh-**toe**)

Petto di bue/brisket
(**boo**-ay)

Piedi di porco/pig's trotters
(pee-**ay**-dee dee porko)

Rognone/kidneys
(ron-**yo**-nay)

Rognoncini/kidneys, small
(ron-**yone**-cheeny)

Salsicce/sausages
(sal-**see**-chay)

Scaloppina/smaller than escalope
(scallow-peena)

Sella/saddle
(**sell**-la)

Trippa/tripe
(treepa)

Pollame/Fowl
(po-**lom**-ay)

Anitra/duck
  (**on**-ee-tra)

Anatroccolo/duckling
  (anna-**trock**-olo)

Beccaccia/woodcock
  (beck-**catch**-a)

Cappone/capon
  (ca-**pony**)

Colomba/pigeon
  (call-**um**-ba)

Fagiano/pheasant
  (fa-**ja**-no)

Gallina/hen
  (gal-**ee**-na)

Gallo/rooster
  (**ga**-lo)

Ghinea/guinea hen
  (geen-**ee**-a)

Oca/goose
  (**aw**-ca)

Pernice/partridge
  (pair-**nee**-chay)

Piccione/pigeon
  (pee-**cho**-nay)

Piccioncino/squab
  (pee-chon-**chee**-no)

Pollo/chicken
  (**paul**-lo)

Quaglia/quail
  (**qua**-lia)

Tacchino/turkey
  (tah-**key**-no)

Pesce, Crostaceo e Mollusco/
Fish, Shellfish and Mollusks

(peh-**shay**, crow-**stachy**-oh,
ay mo-**loose**-co)

Acciughe/anchovies
  (a-chew-gay)

Anguilla/eel
  (ang-gweela)

Aragosta/lobster
  (ara-**ghost**-a)

Aringa/herring
  (a-reengah)

Baccalà/salt cod
  (back-a-**lah**)

Branzino/bass
  (bran-zeeno)

Calamaro/squid
  (calamaro)

Cozze/mussels
  (**cots**-say)

Gamberetti/shrimp
  (gam-**bay**-retty)

Gambero/prawns
  (gam-bay-ro)

Granchio/crab
  (gran-**key**-oh)

Luccio/pike
  (**loo**-cho)

Luccio/sea bass
  (**loo**-cho)

Lumache/snails
  (loo-maw-chay)

Orata/bass
  (or-**ah**-tah)

Ostriche/oysters
  (oss-stree-cay)

Merluzzo/cod
  (mare-**loots**-oh)

Nasello/whiting
  (**na**-sello)

Petonchio/scallop
  (pay-tonkio)

Polipo/octopus
  (**po**-leepo)

Rana/frog
  (rona)

Razza/skate
  (**rats**-sa)

Salmone/salmon
  (sal-moanay)

Sardine/sardine
  (sar-deenay)

Sgombro/mackerel
  (zgumbro)

Sogliola/sole
  (**sole**-yole-a)

Triglia/mullet
  (treelya)

Trote/trout
  (tro-tay)

Vongole/clams
  (vong-**go**-lay)

Metodi per la cottura delle uova/Egg Cooking Methods

(met-**oh**-dee pair la co-toora deli **wove**-ah)

Uova Bollite al fuoco lento/soft boiled
  (**wove**-ah **bo**-lee-tay al fwahco **len**-toe)

Cacciatora, alla/poached in sauce
  (catch-a-tora)

Camicia, in/poached
  (cam-eecha)

Desformado/in ramekins
  (day-for-maud-oh)

Duro/hard boiled
  (**dure**-oh)

Frittata/omelette
  (free-totta)

Fritte/fried
  (**free**-tay)

Griglia, alla/grilled
  (**greel**-ya)

Piatto, al/scrambled
  (**pee**-a-toe)

Legumi or Verdure/Vegetables

(lay-goomy, vair-**doo**-reh)

Aglio cipollina/chive
  all-yo **chee**-pollina

Avena/barley
  (ah-vayna)

Asparago/asparagus
  (a-**spara**-go)

Bietola/beet
  (be-**eh**-tolla)

Carciofo/artichokes
  (car-**chaw**-foe)

Cardone/cardoon
  (car-**doe**-nuh)

Carote/carrots
  (car-**ah**-tay)

Cavolo/cabbage
  (**ca**-vole-oh)

Cavolfiore/cauliflower
  (**ca**-vole-fee-**or**-ay)

Cetriolo/cucumber
  (chay-tree-**all**-oh)

Cipolla/onion
  (**chee**-polla)

Crescione/watercress
  (cray-**show**-nay)

Fava/broad beans
  (**fah**-vah)

Fagiolini/string beans
  (**fah**-joe-leeny)

Finocchio/fennel
(fee-**nock**-yo)

Funghi/mushrooms
(**foong**-gee (as in geek))

Granturco/corn
(**gron**-toorko)

Igname/yam
(een-**yaw**-may)

Lattuga/lettuce
(la-**too**-gah)

Lenticchie/lentils
(len-teak-yah)

Melanzana/eggplant
(may-lanzana)

Pastinaca/parsnip
(paw-**stee**-knocka)

Patata/potatoe
(pa-**tah**-ta)

Peperoni/sweet peppers
(pay-pay-**roni**)

Piselli/peas
(pee-**zel**-ee)

Pomodoro/tomato
(po-mo-**door**-oh)

Porro/leeks
(**pore**-roe)

Prezzemolo/parsley
(pretz-**zay**-mole-oh)

Radicchio/Venetian chicory
(ra-**deekee**-oh)

Rafano/radish
(**ra**-fano)

Rapa/turnip
(**ra**-pa)

Scalogno/shallot
  (scal-**own**-yo)

Sedano/celery
  (**said**-an-oh)

Spinaci/spinach
  (spee-**natch**-ee)

Tartufi/truffles
  (tar-**toofy**)

Zucchini/squash
  (zoo-**keeny**)

Dolce/Desserts

(**dole**-chay)

Biscotto genovese/Genoa pastry tarts
  (**be**-scot-toe jayno-vayzay)

Biscuit tortoni/sponge cake
  (beesquee)

Bonet al cioccolato/chocolate mold
  (bonay-al-chock-o-lato)

Budino di pane/bread pudding
  (boodino-dee pan-**ay**)

Cassata alla Siciliana/pound cake stuffed with
  fruit and ricotta
  (**ca**-sotta alla see-chill-yana)

Castagne al porto/chestnuts with port
  (cas-**tan**-yuh al porto)

Chiacchiere della nonna/trifle cake
  (key-akkery della no-na)

Crema fritta/molded custard
  (crayma-freeta)

Croccante/crunchy cake
  (cro-**con**-tay)

Crostata/tart
  (cro-**stotta**)

Cuscinetti di Teramo/cream puff
  (coo-**she**-netty dee **tare**-amo)

Desfogliota calda/layer cake
  (dess-foal-yahtah callda)

Frittelle/fruit omelette
  (**free**-tell-lay)

Gelato/ice cream
  (jay**lah**toe)

Gelato semi freddo/semi cold ice cream
 (say-me-fraydoe)

Granita di caffé/coffee ice
 (ka-**fay**)

Latte alla Portoghese
 (**lah**-tay alla por-to-gayzay)

Meringa/meringue
 (may-**ring**ah)

Nougat/honey, eggs, nuts in wafers
 (**new**-gah)

Pizza Reale/fancy fruit tart
 (ray-**ah**-lay)

Spuma di cioccolata/whipped chocolate
 pudding
 (spooma dee chocko-lahtah)

Spumone/special ice cream
 (spoo-**moa**ny)

Torta/cake

Tiramisù/chocolate and cheese pudding
 (**tear**-ami-soo)

Zabaglione/frothy egg pudding
 (zabba-**lee**-own-ay)

Zuppa inglese/trifle
 (zoopah ing-glayzay)

Frutta/Fruit

(**froo**-tah)

Albicocca/apricot
 (al-be-**cock**-ka)

Ananasso/pineapple
 (anna-**na**-so)

Anguria/watermelon
 (anguria)

Arancia/orange
 (aran-cha)

Bacca/berry
 (bah-ka)

Banana/banana

Cedro/lime
 (**chay**-dro)

Ciliegia/cherry
 (cheel-**yay**-ja)

Cocomero/watermelon
 (co-**co**-mayro)

Cotogna/quince
 (co-**tone**-ya)

Fichi/figs
 (**fee**-key)

Fragola/strawberry
 (**fra**-go-la)

Lampone/raspberry
 (lam-**pone**-ay)

Limone/lemon
 (lee-moan-ay)

Mandarino/tangerine
 (Mandarino)

Mango/mango

Mela/apple
  (mayla)

Melone/melon
  (may-**loan**-ay)

More/blackberry
  (**mor**ay)

Mortella di palude/cranberry
  (more-tayla dee pa-loo-day)

Olive/olives
  (oh-**lee**-vay)

Pera/pear
  (**pay**-ra)

Pesca/peach
  (peska)

Popone/yellow melon
  (po-**po**-nay)

Prugna/plum
  (**prrune**-ya)

Ribes/currant
  (**ree**-bess)

Ribes nero/black currant
  (near-oh)

Ribes rosso/red currant
  (ross-so)

Susina/plum
  (soo-zina)

Uva/grapes
  (**oo**-va)

Uva secca/raisin
  (secka)

Zucca/pumpkin
  (zoo-ka)

Zuccotto/pumpkin
  (zoo-**cot**-toe)

Formaggi/Cheeses

(for-**mah**-jee)

Asiago
(azy-**a**-go)

Bel Paese
(bell-pie-ayzay)

Cacciocavallo
(catcho-cavallo)

Canestrato
(can-eh-strato)

Crescenza
(cresh-**enza**)

Fior D'Alpe
(**fee**-or **dal**-pay)

Fontina
(fontina)

Gorgonzola
(gorgonzola)

Grana
(grana)

Gruviera
(groove-**yaira**)

Mascarpone
(**mass**-car-**pone**-ay)

Mozzarella
(mots-zar-ella)

Parmigiano
(parmy-janno)

Pecorino Romano
(**pay**-corino)

Provolone
  (pro-vo-loan-ay)

Provatura Romana
  (**prova**-toora)

Ricotta
  (re-**cot**-ta)

Robiole
  (roe-be-**ole**-ay)

Stracchino
  (stra-**kee**no)

Italian Wines

Aglianico del Vulture
(all-**yan**-ee-co del **vool**-to-ray)

Alicante-Bouschet
(al-uh-**con**-tay boo-shay)

Brunello di Montalcino
(brew-**nel**-lo dee mawn-tal-**chee**-no)

Castelli de Jesi
(cas-**stell**-ee de **yay**-zee)

Chianti
(key-on-tee)

Chiaretto
(key-ah-**ret**-o)

Cinqueterre
(**chink**-way-**tair**-ray)

Consorzio
(con-**sorts**-ee-o)

Cortese
(cor-**tay**-zay)

Dolceacqua
(dole-chay-**ack**-wa)

Dolcetto
(dole-**chet**-toe)

Emilia-Romagna
(eh-**mee**-lee-ah ro-**man**-ya)

Frecciarossa
(frech-ya-**ross**-ah)

Ghemme
(**gemm**-ay)

Grignolino
(grin-yo-**leen**-o)

Grumello
(grew-**mell**-o)

Gutturnio
(goo-**toor**-nee-o)

Inferno
(in-**fair**-no)

Ischia
(**isk**-ee-ah)

Montepulciano di Abruzzo
(mawn-tay-pool-**chon**-no dee ah-**broot**-zo)

Oltrepò Pavese
(all-tray-po pa-**vay**-see)

Orvieto
(orv-**yay**-toe)

Passito
(pas-**see**-toe)

Piemonte
(pee-ay-**mawn**-tay)

Recioto
(ray-**chaw**-toe)

Schiava
(ski-**ah**-va)

Sfursat
(sfoor-**tsot**)

Soave
(so-**ah**-vay)

Tignanello
(teen-ya-**nel**-lo)

Tocai
(toe-kigh)

Valpantena
(val-pon-**tay**-na)

Valpolicella
(val-po-lee-**chel**-la)

Venegazzù
(vain-naygot-**tsoo**)

Verdicchio
(vair-**deek**-ee-o)

Verduzzo
(vair-doot-so)

Vernaccia
(vair-**natch**-ah)

Vino Nobile di Montepulciano
(**vee**-no **no**-bee-lay dee mawn-tay-poll-**chon**-no)

French Index

German Index

Italian Index

181